MAMMOTHS
& MASTODONS
of the Ice Age

MAMMOTHS & MASTODONS
of the Ice Age

Adrian Lister

FIREFLY BOOKS

A FIREFLY BOOK

Published by Firefly Books Ltd. 2014

First printing

Publisher Cataloging-in-Publication Data (U.S.)

Lister, Adrian, 1955–
      Mammoths and mastodons of the ice age / Adrian Lister.
[128] p. : col. ill., photos., maps ;   cm.
Includes bibliographical references and index.
Summary: Exploring habits and behaviors of these colossal mammals which roamed throughout Europe, Asia and North America during the ice age, this guide reveals their evolution and extinction, as well as the implication for their surviving cousin, the elephant.
ISBN-13: 978-1-77085-315-7
1. Mammoths. 2. Mastodons. I. Title.
569.67 dc23   QE882.P8L478 2014

Library and Archives Canada Cataloguing in Publication

Lister, Adrian, author
      Mammoths and mastodons of the ice age / Adrian Lister.
Includes photographs of skeletons, casts, tusks and preserved flesh from world-famous collections including those of the Natural History Museum, London.
Includes bibliographical references and index.
ISBN 978-1-77085-315-7 (bound)
      1. Mammoths. 2. Mammoths—Pictorial works. 3. Mastodons. 4. Mastodons—Pictorial works. 5. Glacial epoch.
I. Title.
QE882.P8L57 2014   569'.67   C2013-905979-2

Published in the United States by
Firefly Books (U.S.) Inc.
P.O. Box 1338, Ellicott Station
Buffalo, New York 14205

Published in Canada by
Firefly Books Ltd.
50 Staples Avenue, Unit 1
Richmond Hill, Ontario L4B 0A7

Designed by Mercer Design, London
Front cover image: Shutterstock.com

Reproduction by Saxon Digital Services
Printed China by 1010 Printing International Limited

FSC
www.fsc.org
MIX
Paper from
responsible sources
FSC® C016973

First published by the Natural History Museum
Cromwell Road, London SW7 5BD

Contents

CHAPTER 1
Mammoths and elephants

THE MAMMOTH IS THE ICONIC ANIMAL OF THE ICE AGE. Alongside sabre-tooth cats, cave bears, woolly rhinos and other extinct creatures, mammoths roamed the cold, open landscapes that were also home to our immediate human ancestors. From a geological perspective, this was a world relatively close to ours in time. The Ice Age spanned the last 2.5 million years, but mammoths were still in their heyday only 20,000 years ago, and became extinct as recently as 4,000 years ago. That is less than a hundredth of one per cent of the time since the extinction of the dinosaurs 65 million years ago.

A brief look at a mammoth immediately suggests that it was related to the living elephants. The large size, general body shape, and especially the presence of tusks and trunk, make this clear. In fact, the mammoth was so closely related to the living elephants that it is classified in the same biological family – it **was** an elephant. Elephants today are restricted to two regions of the world – Africa and southern Asia. Both are therefore tropical animals. The mammoth was, in effect, the elephant of the northern hemisphere. With its furry coat and other features, it was adapted to the cooler climates of the north, where conditions during the Ice Age were often more extreme than those today. Yet it was as much an elephant as the living species. Nor was the mammoth the ancestor of today's elephants, as the African and Asian elephants were already living in their tropical ranges while the mammoth roamed the far north. Tracing their remains back through the fossil record, we find that the lineages of the two living elephants and the mammoth all go back around 5 or 6 million years, and diverged from a common ancestor shortly before that time. Elephant evolution began in Africa, where successive species arose and from where several species spread out around the globe.

THE ELEPHANT FAMILY

Elephants are one family within a broader group of mammals known as the Proboscidea – named for their proboscis, or trunk. The story of these animals goes back some 60 million years, beginning, like that of many mammal groups, soon

OPPOSITE With its furry coat, the woolly mammoth was well adapted to the cold of the Ice Age. Other mammoths, however, lived in warmer climates, and all trace their ancestry to early elephants in tropical Africa.

after the extinction of the dinosaurs. The Proboscidea – animals with tusks and trunks and mostly of massive proportions – were widespread around the globe and produced some 200 species over their 60-million-year history (see Chapter 2). One of these species, in Africa around 8–9 million years ago, evolved into the first true elephant, originating the Family Elephantidae.

The earliest elephants have been classified into two types. The larger of the two, around 4 m (13 ft) high, sported four tusks in all – two growing from the lower jaw as well as two in the upper jaw as in living elephants. Its somewhat imposing scientific name is *Stegotetrabelodon*. The other species, the aptly named *Primelephas* ('first elephant'), had only an upper pair of tusks, and stood around 3 m (10 ft) at the shoulder, about the size of a living Asian elephant.

BELOW Mammoths were part of the same family as today's elephants. Here, the woolly mammoth is compared with the three living forms, each showing unique features of the tusks, trunk, hair, head and body.

Woolly mammoth

- Domed head
- Very small ear
- Spiral tusks, males and females
- Sloping back
- Thick fur
- Short tail

African savannah elephant

- Flat head
- Large triangular ear
- Curved tusks, males and females
- Saddle back
- Very sparse fur
- Long tail

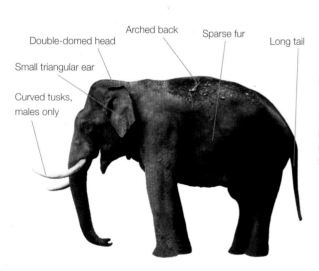

Asian elephant

- Double-domed head
- Small triangular ear
- Curved tusks, males only
- Arched back
- Sparse fur
- Long tail

African forest elephant

- Flat head
- Small rounded ear
- Downward-pointing tusks, males and females
- Straight back
- Very sparse fur
- Long tail

LEFT *Stegotetrabelodon*, the earliest true elephant, had tusks in both its upper and lower jaws – four in all. Its fossils have been found in East Africa in deposits from 7.5 to 4.5 million years ago.

Tusks

Some of the proboscidean species preceding the earliest elephants looked quite similar to them in general appearance. But several features mark out *Stegotetrabelodon* and *Primelephas* as true elephants. The first concerns the tusks themselves. Tusks are, in reality, greatly extended incisor teeth – the biting teeth at the front of the jaw in most mammals, including ourselves. In their original form, therefore, they had the same structure as other teeth – enamel on the outside, dentine on the inside, and a pulp cavity at the centre. This structure is seen in the fossilized tusks of most early proboscideans. But in elephants the enamel has been lost – the tusks are solid dentine, which we know as ivory. Why the enamel was lost is uncertain, but enamel, while very hard, is also more liable to crack. Given the use of tusks in forceful combat, the slightly more pliable dentine was probably less liable to damage.

BELOW Part of the tusk of an American mastodon, showing the enamel covering (to the right of the picture). Toward the tip (to the left) the enamel has worn away to reveal the dentine core.

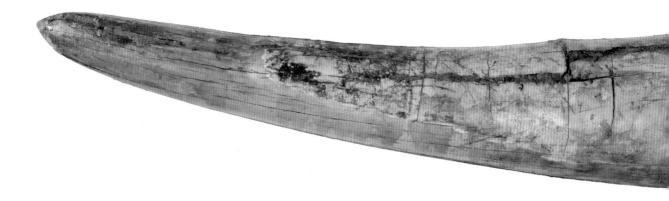

The chewing surface of a typical proboscidean molar tooth prior to the origin of elephants. The pairs of rounded cusps were adapted to crushing soft leaves and fruits.

ABOVE The chewing surface of a typical elephant molar tooth, showing ridges of enamel adapted to grinding coarser plant food including grass.

Diet

The other great innovation of the elephants was linked to a change in diet. Until about 10 million years ago, large areas of Africa were clothed in forest. Gradually, from about that time, global drying of the climate allowed the spread of grasses, patchily at first, but eventually spreading to form the extensive savannahs and grasslands found across much of eastern and southern Africa today. In common with other groups of mammals, the ancestors of the elephants responded to this change by consuming more grass. All proboscideans are entirely herbivorous, but the early forms were adapted to eating largely the leaves of trees, in keeping with their forest or woodland habitat. Reconstructing the diet of extinct species has to rely on fossil remains, and these do not normally include organs like the stomach or intestine, but much can be learned from the form of the teeth and skull.

Teeth

In early proboscideans, the molar teeth comprised a series of rounded cusps which, when the upper and lower teeth met, crushed and ground the food before it was swallowed. This was fine for forest foods like leaves, bark and fruits, which are relatively soft and easy to deal with. Grass leaves, however, are tougher to chew: they contain more fibre and more of the minute silica particles present in many plant cells. To deal with the shift to this coarser food, elephants developed teeth with cusps extended into long ridges that cut past each other and sliced up the grass leaves as the lower jaw swung fore-and-aft. This new method of chewing also affected the form of the jaw muscles and of the jaw bones themselves and, as a result, elephants have relatively short and high heads compared to those of their ancestors (see p.31).

Current scientific research is providing new lines of evidence on the feeding habits of extinct species. One avenue of investigation analyses the carbon component of preserved bones and teeth, deriving ultimately from the plant food consumed by the animal in life. Several forms of carbon atom (called isotopes) exist in nature, and in the Tropics most grasses contain more of one of the rarer varieties (carbon-13) than do the leaves of trees and shrubs. Analysis of the carbon isotopes in fossil proboscidean remains confirm that around 8 million years ago, just as the true elephants were appearing, there was a shift to incorporating significant quantities of grass in their diets.

Family branches

The early elephants in Africa soon diversified into three main branches. The ancestors of today's African elephants diverged first, their earliest known remains coming from East Africa (Kenya and Uganda), and dating to around 6 million years ago. The African elephants are classified under the name *Loxodonta* and never left Africa through their evolutionary history. They are represented today by the African savannah elephant, *Loxodonta africana*, and the smaller and less well-known African forest elephant, *L. cyclotis*, classified by some specialists as two separate species (see p.8).

About a million years later, fossils of the second main branch make their appearance in Africa. These are the earliest representatives of the group that later produced the living Asian elephant. Fossils from East Africa 5 million years old are among the earliest classified as *Elephas*. This branch first became very successful within Africa, and to judge from the fossil record was more numerous and more widespread there than *Loxodonta*, until it died out less than 100,000 years ago and today's African elephant gained its ascendancy.

In the meantime, however, some populations of *Elephas* moved north out of Africa, and east into India where their remains are first seen in deposits of around 3 million years ago. They were the ancestors of today's Asian (or 'Indian') elephants, *E. maximus*, which now extend through the Indian subcontinent and Southeast Asia. Later, another offshoot of the *Elephas* branch also exited Africa and entered Europe, spreading as far as China and Japan: these woodland species were the so-called straight-tusked elephants, some of which survived until around 10,000 years ago.

THE ORIGIN OF MAMMOTHS

The third branch of the elephant family was that of the mammoths. Scientifically named *Mammuthus*, their earliest known remains (*Mammuthus subplanifrons*) date to about 5–6 million years old and were first discovered in South Africa. However, although they originated in Africa, mammoths were, it seems, never very successful there and their remains are rare. Some remains from 3 to 4 million years ago are known from Ethiopia, and finally, at around 2 million years ago in North Africa, the species *Mammuthus africanavus* is found. These early representatives of the mammoth line were tropical animals, not yet showing the cold-climate adaptations of their ultimate descendants the woolly mammoths. Yet, detailed features of their skeletons show that they were already on the mammoth line. These features – which distinguish mammoths from other elephant groups – include the peculiar spiral 'twist' of the tusks, the single dome at the top of the head and the relatively straight enamel ridges of the molars.

BELOW **This massive portion of a lower jaw was found near Bethlehem, and is believed to represent the earliest mammoths out of Africa. The elongated chin (to the bottom of the picture) may have held a pair of lower tusks.**

The fossil record thus demonstrates that not only did all three main branches of the elephant family – the African and Asian elephants and the mammoths – originate on the African continent, they coexisted there, sometimes even in the same regions, for several million years.

Like the Asian elephant lineage, a population of mammoths exited Africa before those left behind went extinct, and the mammoth lineage completed its evolution in other parts of the world. Our best estimate of the date of this emigration is based on the earliest remains outside Africa. Mammoth fossils from Romania and China, of primitive form, are as much as 3.5 million years old, and must date from only shortly after the migration. The route out of Africa was north through what is now the Sahara, but which at times was moister with sufficient growth of vegetation to support the migration of large-mammal populations. From there the route passed through the Middle East, probably in a narrow corridor close to the eastern edge of the Mediterranean, the region now known as the Levant. In the 1950s a remarkable find was unearthed close to the town of Bethlehem. A massive jaw bone 60 cm (2 ft) long, a 2 m (6½ ft) portion of tusk and several isolated molar teeth clearly belonged to a species of elephant. These remains are now preserved at the Natural History Museum in London. Their precise age and identity has been a matter of debate, but recent research has identified them as likely mammoths. Their age remains uncertain, but their primitive form links them to *Mammuthus rumanus*, the earliest European mammoths, named after their place of first discovery in Romania. If this is correct, the Bethlehem finds may be over 3 million years old and would graphically illustrate, from their geographical location in the middle of the Levant, the route of migration of early mammoths out of Africa. The first human migrants would follow some million or more years later.

THE EVOLUTION OF MAMMOTHS

Remains of the earliest Eurasian mammoths, *Mammuthus rumanus*, are rare. Apart from the Romanian finds, a few teeth and partial jaws are known from eastern England, Italy and Bulgaria, and have recently been identified some 8,000 km (5,000 miles) to the east, in northeast China. These remains, 3 million or so years old, show that once out of Africa, mammoths spread rapidly across the Eurasian continent. However, their range at that time remained relatively southern. Remains of fossil plants found with the earliest European mammoths show that they were still living in a relatively warm, wooded environment, and analysis of their tooth wear shows that they were incorporating quantities of tree and shrub browse in their diet along with some grasses.

The transformation from this stage to the Ice Age adapted woolly mammoth, *Mammuthus primigenius,* forms one of the most convincing examples of evolutionary change known from the entire fossil record of land animals. Around 2.5 million years ago the Ice Age began – the geological period known as the

RIGHT Maps showing the origin and spread of mammoth, *Mammuthus* species. In the crucial period 2–1 million years ago, *Mammuthus trogontherii* arose in east Asia, spread to Europe and began to displace *M. meridionalis*, and colonised North America, giving rise to *M. columbi*. Purple arrows: migration; red arrows: migration and evolution into new species.

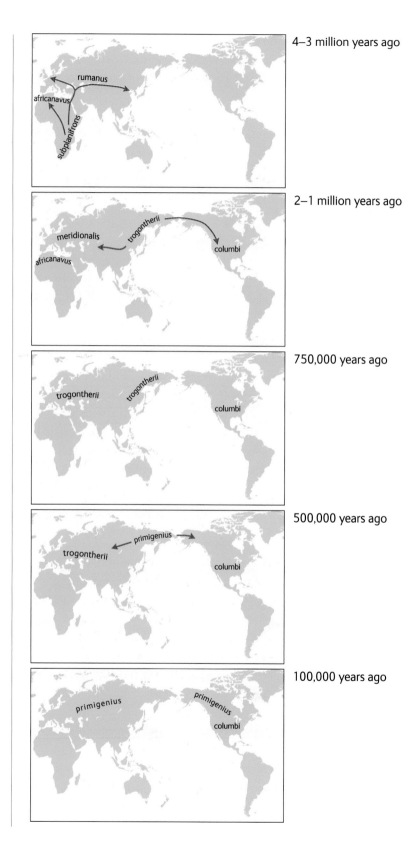

4–3 million years ago

2–1 million years ago

750,000 years ago

500,000 years ago

100,000 years ago

Quaternary (see Chapter 3). Overall through this period, the climate cooled, and as a result forests gave way to open habitats in many parts of the world. Many animal species were forced to shift their distribution, adapt to the new conditions, or face extinction. In the case of the mammoth, adaptation happened in stages, taking the lineage through a series of species in response to changing environments. This evolutionary response has been traced mainly through a study of preserved molar teeth, with changes also observed in the skull, jaws and other parts of the skeleton. Other aspects of the animals' anatomy require informed guesswork, as degradable tissues such as the hair and trunk (which is purely muscular and contains no bones) are directly known only in the latest woolly mammoths (see Chapter 4), by which time the evolutionary transformation was complete. It is reasonable to assume, however, that the earliest mammoths out of Africa would have had a sparse hair covering similar to that of the living elephants, and that their fur thickened and lengthened progressively as they moved north and into colder climates.

ABOVE **The early mammoth** *Mammuthus meridionalis* **held sway in Europe for over a million years. It lived in a relatively mild climate and its food included tree and shrub browse as well as grasses.**

Mammoths begin to adapt

After the *Mammuthus rumanus* stage, mammoth remains become much more abundant in the fossil record. The next species in the chain is scientifically named *Mammuthus meridionalis* but is informally known as the 'southern mammoth' or 'ancestral mammoth'. This species was still relatively southern in its range, but is represented at many fossil localities in Europe, southern Russia and China. The remains include complete skeletons, showing that this was an animal of large size even by mammoth standards – measurements of its shoulder height average around 4 m (13 ft), allowing estimation of its body weight in life of about 10 tonnes. This can be compared to 3.2 m (10 ft 6 in) and 6 tonnes for a large bull African elephant, the largest land mammal alive today. Its teeth also show advancement over *Mammuthus rumanus*: the number of enamel ridges in its back molars, for example, had increased from 10 to 14 or so, providing greater resistance to wear from abrasive plant food. *Mammuthus meridionalis* was a highly successful species that endured from 2.5 to 0.75 million years ago, or almost 2 million years.

Important recent discoveries in northeast China suggest that the next stage in mammoth evolution happened in that region around 1.7 million years ago. Molars were found that proved to be markedly more advanced than contemporary *Mammuthus meridionalis* in Europe: the number of enamel ridges had increased to 17 or 18 and, even more significantly, the crown of the molar had become much higher. This change marks the largest single shift in evolution toward the woolly mammoth condition. Consuming ever greater quantities of grass increased the rate of tooth wear, so to maintain the same lifespan before the teeth wore out, the molar crowns almost doubled in height. The increased wear came about not only because of the tougher nature of grass food but also because the more an animal feeds on plants close to the ground, as opposed to browsing tree leaves, the more soil grit it picks up with its food, adding to the abrasion of the teeth. Starting about 2 million years ago, northern China experienced an increasingly seasonal climate, with very cold winters and the spread of a largely open, grassy habitat. These changes probably triggered evolution in a local population of *Mammuthus meridionalis*, resulting in the formation of the new species *Mammuthus trogontherii*, sometimes known as the 'steppe mammoth'.

ABOVE Mammoth molars in side view, showing increase in crown height. Top: *Mammuthus rumanus* from Bethlehem, some 3–4 million years old, with low crown. Bottom: *Mammuthus primigenius* from Siberia, some 50,000 years old, with high crown.

This species showed further anatomical changes. The high tooth crowns had to be sunk into the jaw bones so these deepened, resulting in a relatively taller head. Recent study of a *Mammuthus trogontherii* skeleton from China indicates that the tail had shortened as a likely adaptation to cold climate (see Chapter 4). However, the species retained the very large size of its immediate ancestor, with shoulder heights of up to 4 m (13 ft) and a body weight up to 10 tonnes. After its origin in China, *Mammuthus trogontherii* spread to other regions of Eurasia as climates cooled and habitats opened. By a million years ago it had arrived in southern Russia, and by around 800,000 years ago in central Europe. On arrival in these regions it encountered remnant populations of *Mammuthus meridionalis*, but these soon became extinct.

Origin of woolly mammoths

Mammuthus trogontherii was the first mammoth species to extend its range across the Arctic Circle. Abundant remains of this species, mostly isolated teeth, tusks and bones, were unearthed along the banks of the Kolyma River in the

ABOVE The skeleton of a steppe mammoth, *Mammuthus trogontherii*, unearthed in Serbia in 2009. The pelvis is on the left, with vertebral column and ribs emerging to the right. The hind limbs, folded beneath the pelvis, indicate the animal died in a crouching position.

primigenius

trogontherii

meridionalis

rumanus

ABOVE The evolution of the mammoth illustrated by its teeth. Over three million years, from *Mammuthus rumanus* through *M. meridionalis* and *M. trogontherii* to the woolly mammoth *M. primigenius*, the number of enamel ridges in the last molars increased threefold, from 8 to around 24.

far northeast of Siberia in the 1960–70s, and dated to 1.2–0.8 million years ago. It was here, in the extreme environments of northern Siberia, that the final stage of evolution to the woolly mammoth took place. The cold, treeless environments of the Ice Age had come earliest to that region (by about 2.5 million years ago) and were most persistent there. These conditions undoubtedly account for the earliest appearance of woolly mammoth fossils there, in deposits of the Kolyma region around 800,000–600,000 years old. The molar teeth were even higher-crowned and had now reached 23–24 enamel plates in the back molars – an extreme adaptation to grazing low-growing grasses and other herbs, and signalling the arrival of the woolly mammoth species, *Mammuthus primigenius*.

Like the steppe mammoth before it, the woolly mammoth expanded its range during glacial episodes, when its preferred habitat spread over vast areas. The timing of its first arrival in Europe is uncertain, but it had certainly arrived by early in the penultimate glaciation – around 190,000 years ago – and may have encroached into the region significantly earlier. There it encountered remnant populations of steppe mammoth, and the two may have partitioned habitats for a while, the steppe mammoth in slightly warmer, partly wooded areas, the woolly mammoth in more open, colder areas. The two species may even have interbred to a degree. However, by the last glaciation (starting around 100,000 years ago) the woolly mammoth had prevailed.

AMERICAN MAMMOTHS

When mammoths first arrived in northeast Siberia a million or more years ago, they found themselves on the threshold of the New World. The migration route of mammoths into North America, as for many other species including humans, was via the Bering land bridge that formed whenever the sea level dropped below a certain point (see p.50). Today, the coasts of northeast Siberia and northwest Alaska are separated by only 82 km (51 miles) of seaway – the Bering Strait, with a maximum depth of less than 50 m (about 165 ft). Therefore, during glacial episodes, when global sea level dropped by up to 120 m (nearly 400 ft), a broad area of land connected the two continents. The timing of migration of mammoths into the Americas can be estimated from the earliest mammoth fossils known from there. These remains are rare but widely dispersed, ranging from Florida, USA, to Saskatchewan, Canada, and are in the range 1.7–1.5 million years ago.

Until recently it was assumed that the mammoth species crossing into the New World was *Mammuthus meridionalis*, since that species was the only one known in Eurasia in the relevant time period, between around 2.0 and 1.5 million years ago. This idea is problematic, however, since remains of *Mammuthus meridionalis* have never been found in northern Siberia. The species was evidently not adapted to arctic climes and so was not in a position to be able to cross the Bering land connection. However, the discovery of *Mammuthus trogontherii* in northeast China at around 1.7 million years ago (see above) has provided an alternative solution. In the crucial region of northeast Siberia, close to the migration route, *Mammuthus trogontherii* are dated to around 1.2 million years and they may well have been there earlier – there are no fossil-yielding deposits of the preceding interval in the area.

It therefore seems likely that *Mammuthus trogontherii* was the species that first entered the New World. This idea is supported not only by its occurrence more than a million years ago on the Siberian side, but by the finding of very similar fossils of like age from the Yukon (Canada) on the North American side. A final piece of evidence is provided by the form of the North American mammoths themselves; in their large body size and tooth morphology, *Mammuthus columbi*, the Columbian mammoth, is strikingly similar to the Eurasian *Mammuthus trogontherii*. From Alaska and the Yukon it moved south, eventually occupying a range encompassing most of the continental USA and Mexico, and extending

ABOVE The fragment of molar tooth used by Scottish palaeontologist Hugh Falconer to name the Columbian mammoth in 1857. The specimen, 20 cm (8 in) long, is from Georgia, USA, and is labelled in Falconer's handwriting.

BELOW This huge molar tooth (right), with attached skull bone, of a Columbian mammoth from Texas, USA, measures 32×27×13 cm (12½×10¾×5 in). An equivalent molar of woolly mammoth (left), to the same scale, graphically illustrates the size difference between the species.

RIGHT The Columbian mammoth shared the high head dome, sloping back and twisted tusks of its woolly cousin, but at 4 m (13 ft 1 in) high was substantially larger. Its hair covering is unknown but was probably less than in the woolly mammoth.

occasionally as far south as Costa Rica. There is no evidence that mammoths ever crossed the isthmus into South America, however. From its origin at around 1.5 million years ago, *Mammuthus columbi* held sway over the southern half of the North American continent.

With the subsequent origin of the woolly mammoth, *Mammuthus primigenius*, in the Beringian area, a second wave of migration into the New World was inevitable. The timing of this event is uncertain, but by the penultimate glaciation around 150,000 years ago, if not earlier, woolly mammoths were spreading across the northern part of the North American continent. Their remains are particularly abundant in Alaska and the Yukon, with other finds across Canada and in northern US states such as Maine and Wisconsin.

Woolly and Columbian mammoths

Did the woolly and Columbian mammoths ever meet and, if so, how did they interact? The ranges of the two species, at roughly the Canada/US border, seem to have approached very closely, if not overlapped. At the Hot Springs Mammoth Site in South Dakota, most remains are of Columbian mammoth, but a few woolly mammoth fossils have also been found. However, it is not clear if the species were in the vicinity at precisely the same time, since the woolly mammoth remains are in a higher rock stratum than the Columbians. Perhaps the boundary between the species shifted north and south as Ice Age climates oscillated.

More recent evidence of interaction between the species has come in the form of ancient DNA (see Chapter 4). Very few Columbian mammoths have so far yielded DNA, but one individual, a male skeleton from Huntingdon, Utah, dated to around 13,000 years ago, produced a DNA sequence that, surprisingly, was identical to that of woolly mammoths to the north, suggesting that it had inherited woolly mammoth genes along the female line. Yet in its size and tooth form, the animal looked like a Columbian mammoth. The most likely explanation is that Columbian and woolly mammoths occasionally interbred where their ranges met and, in particular, the larger Columbian males may have mated with the smaller woolly females. Such an idea finds a parallel among modern African elephants, where there is genetic evidence of the larger savannah bulls mating with the smaller forest females. Such occasional interbreeding does not, according to most biologists today, negate the status of the animals as separate species, as long as the level of interbreeding is not such as to merge the populations into one homogeneous form.

The likelihood of interbreeding between Columbian and woolly mammoths may explain another long-standing puzzle: the status of so-called 'Jeffersonian mammoths', fossils which have been given the scientific name *Mammuthus jeffersoni* and which have been mainly identified in the midwest region of the USA. These animals were as large as Columbian mammoths, but have molars that are intermediate in form between those of Columbian and woolly mammoths. Could they represent hybrid individuals between the two species?

DWARFING OF THE GIANTS

In September 1904 the intrepid English palaeontologist Dorothea Bate made a remarkable discovery at a site on the northeast coast of Crete. There she uncovered fossilized molar teeth that were evidently from some kind of elephant, but of an

RIGHT The area of northwest Crete where Dorothea Bate discovered fossil remains now recognised as those of pygmy mammoth. The site is the location of a former cave system in which the bones had accumulated.

RIGHT The upper arm bone (humerus) of a pygmy mammoth exposed in a sediment block. Its surface has eroded to reveal the spongy interior. At 33 cm (13 in), the length of the humerus is a quarter that of its likely mainland ancestor.

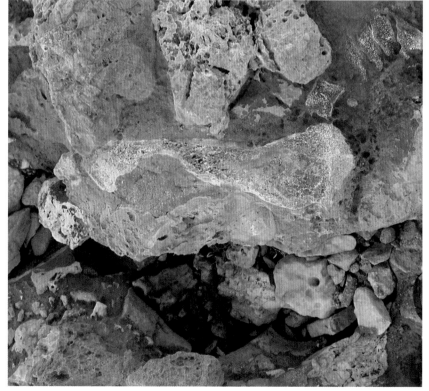

astonishingly small size. Back in London she pondered her finds. These were not the first dwarf elephant teeth found in the Mediterranean – examples had been known from Malta since the mid-nineteenth century, and Bate herself had discovered similarly diminutive remains in Cyprus. But the Cretan teeth were different, and Bate named them a new species – *Elephas creticus*. She very presciently noted that, of possible mainland ancestors, they most closely resembled (though very much smaller) the molars of the species then known as *Elephas meridionalis*. However, because Bate found only teeth and no limb bones, she was not able to give a reliable estimate of the size of the dwarfed species.

New evidence

Just over 100 years later, an expedition from the Natural History Museum in London, armed with Bate's original notes from her travels, relocated the site where she had discovered the dwarf remains. There they found further examples of the diminutive teeth and, most significantly, the first limb element of the species, an upper arm bone (humerus) embedded in the rock. The humerus was a mere 33 cm (13 in) long, from which could be calculated a living shoulder height of barely over a metre (3¼ ft) and a body weight of around 300 kg (660 lb). Moreover, the bone was clearly of an adult animal, not a juvenile that had yet to complete its

ABOVE The molar of the Cretan pygmy mammoth (bottom), 14 cm (5½ in) long, compared to that of its likely ancestor *Mammuthus meridionalis* (top) (specimen from Norfolk, England). The low crown height (below, right) suggests a relationship between the two.

BELOW Artist's reconstruction
of an adult dwarf mammoth
from Crete, *Mammuthus
creticus*. At just over a metre
tall, it was a quarter the height
of its mainland ancestor.

growth. From the tooth remains, the team were able to confirm Bate's hunch that the closest relative of the Cretan dwarf was the mainland species *meridionalis*, the fossil elephant which after Bate's time had been shown to be an early member of the Eurasian mammoth lineage, and is now known as *Mammuthus meridionalis* (see above). This was based especially on the low height of the molar crown, strongly suggesting that its mainland ancestor was the early species of mammoth, *Mammuthus meridionalis* or perhaps even its predecessor *Mammuthus rumanus*, the first mammoth in Europe. Given the known geological range of these species, a population of one of them must have arrived in Crete at least 0.75 million, and maybe as much as 3 million, years ago.

The Cretan mammoths, now renamed *Mammuthus creticus*, were the smallest mammoths ever to evolve. Elephants of similar size are known from Cyprus, Malta and Sicily, but they are all derived from a different stock, the straight-tusked elephant *Palaeoloxodon,* a relative of the living Asian elephant (see above). One other Mediterranean island has yielded fossils identified as a dwarf mammoth – this is *Mammuthus lamarmorai* from Sardinia, and its sparse remains suggest a mammoth that was dwarfed but not to the degree seen on Crete – its body weight can be estimated at around 750 kg (1650 lb). With the possible exception of Malta and Sicily, the dwarfed species on different islands must represent separate colonization events

from the mainland, since none of the other islands was ever connected to another. *Mammuthus lamarmorai*, moreover, looks like it evolved from a later mammoth species than *Mammuthus creticus*, perhaps the mainland species *Mammuthus trogontherii*, and therefore the colonization must have happened significantly later – probably sometime between 700,000 and 200,000 years ago.

American dwarf mammoths

On the other side of the world, island dwarfs evolved from yet another mammoth species – the Columbian mammoth, *Mammuthus columbi*. Numerous remains of diminutive mammoths – aptly named *Mammuthus exilis* – have been found on the California Channel Islands, a small group of islands currently around 30 km (19 miles) from the coast near Los Angeles. Until 20 years ago only isolated teeth, tusks and bones were known, but in 1994 an almost complete individual was exposed on the island of Santa Rosa. It was the skeleton of an ageing male, complete except for one tusk and small portions of its skull and backbone. The animal had evidently died lying on its left side and been covered by sand. Most of the dwarfed mammoths from the Channel Islands date from between 15,000 and 13,000 years ago, and so are much later than those from the Mediterranean. They also bring to three the species of mainland mammoths that independently produced dwarfed island descendants.

The extent of dwarfing in island mammoths (and other elephants) is extraordinary, and proportionally far exceeds that in other kinds of mammals that became reduced on islands, such as hippos and deer. The three ancestral species, *Mammuthus meridionalis*, *M. trogontherii* and *M. columbi* were all of large size even by mammoth standards, rendering the degree of dwarfing all the more remarkable. Each was around 4 m (13 ft) tall and weighed up to 10 tonnes in the adult – so the Cretan dwarf at around 1 m (3¼ ft) and 300 kg (660 lb) was only 3% the weight of its mainland ancestor. For the smallest Santa Rosa animals the figure is around 5% and on Sardinia 8%.

Why does dwarfing happen?

The most likely cause of dwarfing was the limited amount of forage available in the restricted land area of a small island – reduced further on islands with a rocky interior hosting less suitable vegetation and perhaps inaccessible to the mammoths.

RIGHT The excavation of the first complete skeleton of a dwarf mammoth, on Santa Rosa island off California in 1994. The skull and tusk are exposed beneath the grid on the right, while the excavator points to the animal's pelvis.

Small individuals – with lesser food requirement – would be more likely to survive, and so would be favoured by natural selection. Another factor is the frequent lack of large ground predators (such as wolves or big cats) on islands, so potential prey animals lost another reason to be large – defence against attack. A final possible explanation is that smaller animals reproduce at a younger age, so in a challenging environment could have been at an advantage against slower-developing larger individuals.

Whatever the cause, the initial colonizers of the islands must have been full-sized individuals of the mainland species. How did they get there? In the case of some island mammals, lowered sea levels during Ice Age glaciations connected the island to the mainland, so when sea levels rose again a population of the species might be cut off as the island re-formed, and the process of dwarfing could begin. This, however, does not seem likely for the three islands known to have hosted dwarf mammoths, since in each case the seaway to the mainland was too deep to form a land bridge even during glacial episodes. The animals must therefore have arrived by swimming. The lowered sea level would still have assisted, by narrowing the distance to be crossed: in the case of Sardinia, for example, there was a land connection to Corsica and from there only 10 km (just over 6 miles) of open sea to mainland Italy. Similarly in California, sea-level drop united the present-day islands of Santa Rosa, San Miguel and Santa Cruz into a single larger island only

10 km from the mainland. Crete is much further from the mainland of Greece (to the west) or Turkey (to the east), but in either direction a chain of islands would have allowed the animals to 'island hop' with a seaway of no more than 20 km (12½ miles) between any two. Living elephants are excellent swimmers, using all four limbs as paddles and their trunk as a snorkel, and animals have been recorded swimming to islands up to 48 km (30 miles) offshore. Mammoths presumably had similar capabilities, and would have been attracted by the aroma of vegetation from the island, although successful establishment of a viable island population was probably a rare event.

If a population became established on an island, however, the beginnings of dwarfing would have been aided by the fact that mammoths were apparently quite flexible in body size. For example, among woolly mammoths, fossils from several sites show populations which, while not truly dwarfed, were no more than 2 m (6½ ft) in shoulder height (compared to the usual 3 m or 10 ft in that species). Examples include the mammoth population of Wrangel Island in the Arctic Ocean (see Chapter 5), but also some mainland ones, such as the family groups of mammoths discovered in ancient flood deposits west of Moscow. In the California Channel Islands, where mammoths have been found at more than 140 sites, there is variation in size among the remains. At some sites the mammoths are almost as large as the 4 m (13 ft) high animals of the mainland. At others, the bones indicate individuals ranging from 1.2 to 1.8 m (4 to 6 ft) in height. These remains may demonstrate the process of dwarfing – the largest ones representing the initial colonizers, progressively smaller ones reflecting different stages in the evolutionary sequence. However, it is difficult to be sure of this, because most of the remains are poorly dated. Some of the large individuals might represent later, unsuccessful attempts at colonization even after the dwarfs had evolved. In general, we have little idea how long dwarfing took for any of the diminutive populations – it could have been thousands, tens of thousands, or in some cases even hundreds of thousands of years. Only the discovery and dating of more fossils from the islands will start to resolve this question.

CHAPTER 2
Tusks and trunks

MAMMOTHS AND ELEPHANTS COMPRISE ONE RELATIVELY SMALL FAMILY within the larger mammalian grouping known as the Proboscidea – animals with trunk and tusks. The Proboscidea (or proboscideans, more informally) are in turn one of the 20 or so major living groups of mammals known scientifically as orders, others being the primates, whales, bats and so on. With only two or three surviving species, the Proboscidea are one of the least diverse orders, compared to rodents, for example, with more than 2,000 species. Over their 60-million-year history, however, the Proboscidea produced around 200 diverse species, almost all now extinct.

THE PROBOSCIDIANS

The earliest known fossil proboscidean is named *Eritherium*, and was discovered as recently as 2009. Unearthed in phosphate deposits in Morocco, it is around 60 million years old. The remains of around 15 individuals were found, the fossils comprising mostly parts of skulls, jaws and teeth. At around 5 kg (11 lb) in body weight – the size of a large rabbit – *Eritherium* was small by proboscidean standards but still marks a significant size increase over the shrew-like mammals that preceded it. Most importantly, it has tell-tale signs in its anatomy that it was on the proboscidean line. Although it lacked a trunk and did not look much like its later descendants, it did have enlarged incisor teeth, the precursors of tusks.

The subsequent evolution of the Proboscidea is marked by dramatic further increase in size, lengthening of the legs, enlargement of the skull, and the growth of up to four massive tusks. The weight of the head – up to a tonne in a living elephant, including the heavy, forwardly

OPPOSITE Over its 60 million year history, the Proboscidea produced some 200 diverse species. Among them, the deinotheres had a block-like skull and unique, backwardly-curved lower tusks.

BELOW The fragmentary skull and teeth of *Eritherium*, the oldest known proboscidean, some 60 million years old, from Morocco. The small size of the specimen, a mere 4 cm (1½ in) long, contrasts dramatically with later members of the group.

RIGHT Evolutionary tree of the proboscideans. The first true elephants, *Primelephas* and *Stegotetrabelodon*, led to three branches – mammoths (*Mammuthus*), Asian elephants (*Elephas*) and African elephants (*Loxodonta*), while the mastodon (*Mammut*) had a much more ancient ancestry. Ma = millions of years ago.

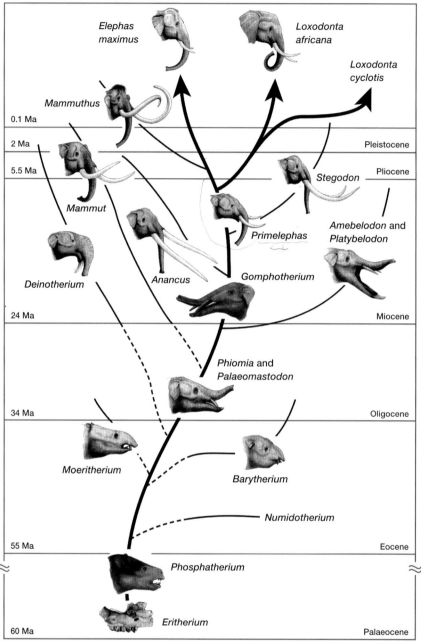

Phylogeny of Proboscidea

protruding tusks – could not have been supported, still less raised and lowered, on the end of a long neck. So the neck became greatly shortened during the course of proboscidean evolution, but this created another problem: with the mouth 3 m (10 ft) from the ground, how was the animal to feed and drink? This problem was solved by the evolution of the trunk, a mobile, muscular organ by which the animal could procure and raise food and water to its mouth. These changes did not happen in succession, but in tandem and progressively through time.

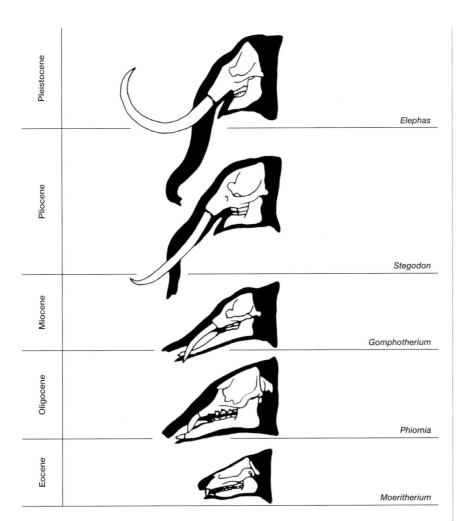

Pleistocene

Pliocene

Miocene

Oligocene

Eocene

Elephas

Stegodon

Gomphotherium

Phiomia

Moeritherium

LEFT Stages in the evolution of the proboscidean head. As the body enlarged, the tusks lengthened and the trunk developed, the skull and jaw became higher and shorter.

Moeritherium

By 40 million years ago, proboscidean evolution had produced a creature the size of a large pig. This was *Moeritherium*, a successful genus that endured until around 32 million years ago and lived around the shores of the former Tethys Sea – the precursor of the Mediterranean. Still lacking a trunk it had, however, developed its side upper and lower incisors into incipient tusks. *Moeritherium* had a barrel-shaped body and short legs but its limb bones were of a distinctly elephantine type. It was very probably semi-aquatic in habitat, rather like a small version of a living hippopotamus.

An affinity to water was a frequent theme in proboscidean evolution. This observation, based originally on fossil occurrences, received unexpected support from a study of the kidney in foetal elephants. Researchers observed the presence of microscopic tubes called nephrostomes, part of a water-balance system generally seen only in aquatic animals, and suggestive of an aquatic or semi-aquatic ancestry for the proboscideans. It may not be coincidental that the closest living

ABOVE *Moeritherium* lived from 40–32 million years ago and had the appearance of a small hippopotamus. The side incisors had enlarged to form incipient tusks.

BELOW The fossilised lower jaw of *Palaeomastodon* shows five chewing teeth in place at one time. This 40 cm (1 ft 4 in) long specimen, some 30 million years old, is from the Fayum, Egypt.

relatives of the Proboscidea are the dugongs and sea-cows. These large mammals, superficially seal-like in appearance but slow-moving and entirely herbivorous, are fully aquatic, inhabiting marine coastal areas and rivers in the Tropics. Their relationship to elephants is beyond doubt, based on similarities of their DNA and their anatomy. It is therefore not unlikely that the common ancestor from which both they and the proboscideans sprang was aquatic or semi-aquatic in habit.

After *Moeritherium*, size increase continued, and proboscideans arose that were longer in the leg and more terrestrially adapted. These and many of the fossil forms over the next 30 million years or so are sometimes casually termed 'mastodons' (alternative spelling: 'mastodonts'). This word, meaning 'breast-tooth',

BELOW A skull of *Palaeomastodon*, a close relative of *Phiomia*. Although damaged on top, the 1 m (3 ft 3 in) long skull shows the complete tooth-row as well as the elongated 'chin' which housed the flattened lower tusks.

was coined by the celebrated French anatomist Baron Cuvier in 1806, in reference to the hemispherical shape of the molar cusps. Cuvier originally applied the name to molars of the celebrated American mastodon, and the term is best restricted to that form and its close relatives, which will be dealt with later.

Phiomia

From 35 to 25 million years ago, still in the Tethys region of North Africa, we find the related forms *Phiomia* and *Palaeomastodon*, now 2 m (6½ ft) high at the shoulder and of a distinctly elephantine shape, with short upper and lower tusks (the lower pair flattened) and probably a short trunk. The trunk of a proboscidean cannot be directly observed in the fossil record, because it contains no bones. However, the presence of a single, enlarged nasal

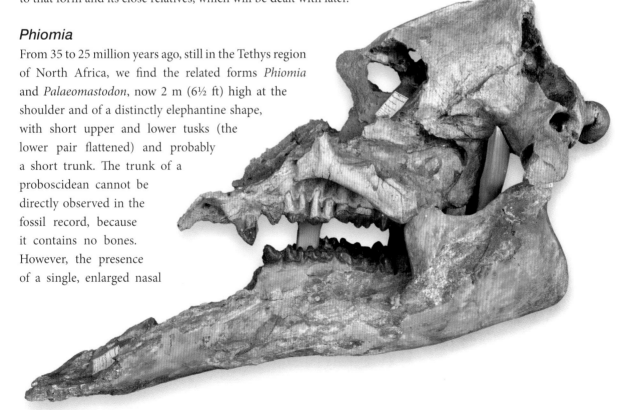

RIGHT The skull and lower jaw of the Miocene proboscidean *Gomphotherium*. The single nasal opening, signifying the presence of a trunk, is visible on top. Both upper and lower tusks are present, giving a total length of 1.4 m (4 ft 7 in).

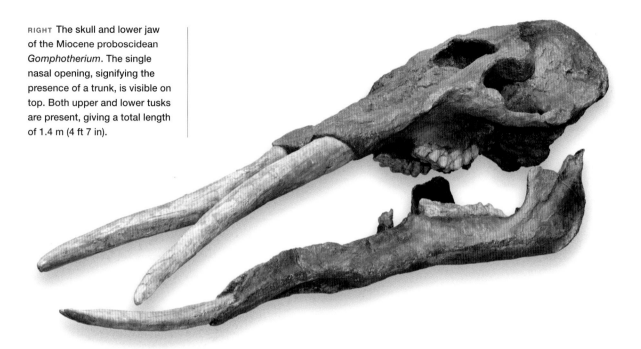

opening at the front of the skull reveals the existence of a trunk, which is formed anatomically from a fusion of the nose and upper lip. *Phiomia* is believed to have inhabited open woodland with ready access to water.

Gomphotheres

The most widespread and successful group of proboscideans were the gomphotheres. The genus *Gomphotherium*, after which the group is named, was a kind of standard-order gomphothere from which later, more bizarre forms

BELOW Reconstruction of a scene in Spain some 16 million years ago. A group of *Gomphotherium* has come down to the river to drink, while a family of pigs (*Bunolistriodon*) forages on the other side.

developed. It arose around 20 million years ago and endured for some 15 million years. Dispersing widely from Africa, its remains are found also in Europe and Asia, and around 15 million years ago it entered North America, where it rapidly spread across the continent. Almost the size of an Asian elephant, *Gomphotherium* had a well-developed trunk, to judge from its long legs, short neck, and the size and position of its nasal opening. Its head was longer and lower than that of a modern elephant, with extended jaws bearing the upper and lower tusks. *Gomphotherium* is believed to have been a browsing animal of open woodland, and its tusks frequently show fine scratches running lengthways close to the tip, interpreted as evidence of bark-stripping behaviour as in living elephants.

In its dentition, *Gomphotherium* shows one key advance over the *Phiomia* stage, one that characterized most later proboscideans and developed to an extreme in the true elephants. Early proboscideans, like many other groups of

BELOW The lower jaw of a mastodon, showing a stage in the evolution of tooth replacement. As the tooth at the front (bottom of page) wore out, a new tooth erupted at the back. No more than three (as here) of the six teeth are in use at a time.

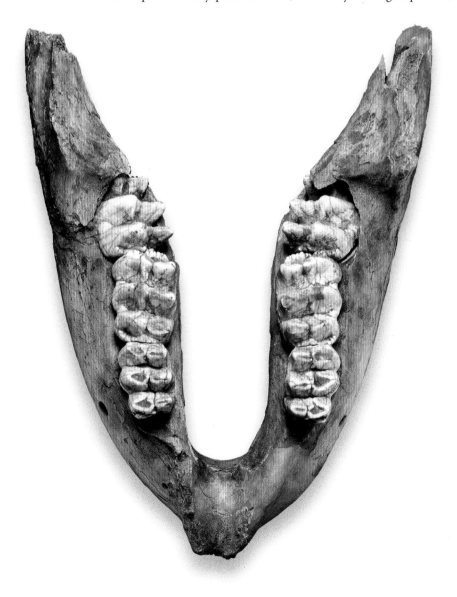

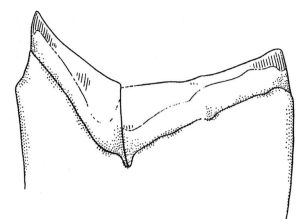

ABOVE Close-up of the end of the flattened 'shovel' tusks in a *Platybelodon* fossil. The sharpened, V-shaped edge suggests they were used to cut vegetation in a side-to-side sawing motion.

BELOW Reconstruction of *Amebelodon*, a celebrated 'shovel-tusker' from the Miocene of North America. The trunk (which recent research suggests was not as flattened as shown here) would have worked to hold vegetation against the cutting edges of the lower tusks.

herbivorous mammals, had six chewing teeth in each jaw. By adulthood they had all erupted and remained there for the rest of the animal's life. With the enlargement of the teeth and shortening of the head in later proboscideans, however, a system of sequential tooth replacement developed. As the front tooth wore out with use, another erupted at the back of the row, each successive tooth larger than the preceding one to keep pace with the growth of the animal. In this way the six teeth were still used, but not all at the same time. In the case of *Gomphotherium*, there were typically around three molars present in the jaw at any point in the animal's life: numbers 1-2-3, 2-3-4, 3-4-5, and finally 4-5-6.

Gomphotheres produced many species and spread widely across the globe, including the only incursion of the Proboscidea into South America. As plate tectonics moved that continent close to North America about 5 million years ago, many mammal groups invaded from the north, including gomphothere proboscideans, and these subsequently gave rise to endemic South American species.

Shovel-tuskers

Among the most celebrated of fossil proboscideans are the so-called 'shovel-tuskers' *Amebelodon* and *Platybelodon*. In these forms, the slightly flattened lower tusks of *Phiomia* and *Gomphotherium* became hugely exaggerated to form two massive, strongly flattened tusks placed side by side to form a shape akin to a

shovel. The function of these massive organs has been the subject of much debate. The animals have generally been reconstructed as wading in shallow ponds and lakes, rooting out marshy vegetation. The discovery of tusks with polished tips confirms that this was probably one mode of feeding for *Amebelodon*, but other individuals showed scratches and cutting edges on their tusks, indicating that the animals had broader diets, also utilizing leaves, bark and twigs of trees. In *Platybelodon* a V-shaped sharpened tip suggests that the tusks were used like saws for cutting through tough vegetation in a side-to-side motion. In all of this the tusks would have worked together with the trunk, which to judge from an *Amebelodon* skull recently described from Florida was long, massive and highly muscular.

ABOVE The swamp forests of the Miocene were home to *Deinotherium*, an early proboscidean with remarkable downwardly-curved lower tusks. Sharing this habitat were early relatives of the horse, and the mongoose (in the foreground).

Deinotheres

Another bizarre, early offshoot within the Proboscidea were the deinotheres. They arose around 25 million years ago and throughout their long, 20-million-year history they changed relatively little apart from an increase in size, the largest forms reaching 4 m (13 ft) in shoulder height. Their range remained relatively limited, not extending beyond the tropical and temperate regions of the Old World. Lacking upper tusks, their most prominent feature was their unique, backwardly curving lower tusks, thought to have been used for bark-stripping trees. Their nostril indicates a trunk of sorts, placed high on the skull. Their teeth remained relatively simple and they did not develop the horizontal tooth replacement system of other groups.

Stegodons

The stegodons are another interesting group, because they were long thought to be the immediate ancestors of the true elephants, although they are now considered by many researchers to be more distantly related to them. If so, then the features they show in common with elephants must have evolved separately. These include the molar teeth, which became greatly elongated with multiplication of the enamel

BELOW Reconstruction of *Stegodon*, a proboscidean sometimes considered ancestral to elephants. It was widespread in Asia from around 12 million years ago, entering Africa only later, opposite to the migration of many other groups.

ridges, and an extreme replacement system with only one or two teeth in the jaw at any one time. Stegodons reached 3.5 m (11½ ft) in height, had a relatively low forehead compared to elephants, but carried massive upper tusks that stretched nearly 3 m (10 ft) in front of the animal, almost touching the ground. Another peculiar feature was that the tusks ran parallel and very close together so that the trunk cannot have hung between them as in elephants but must have draped over them to the left or right.

Stegodons are of further interest in that, like some elephant and mammoth species (see Chapter 1), they produced dwarfed forms on islands. Fossils of diminutive stegodons have been found on several islands of Southeast Asia. On the island of Flores (one of a chain of small islands east of Java) there is evidence of two waves of colonization and dwarfing. The smallest stegodon species on Flores is almost a million years old and had an estimated body weight of about 300 kg (660 lb). It appears to have died out but was replaced by a second species that dwarfed to around 500 kg (1100 lb). The latter form survived until only 12,000 years ago and was a contemporary of the celebrated dwarfed human species,

BELOW The skull of *Stegodon*, with its impressive 3 m (9 ft 10 in) long tusks. These are so close together that the trunk cannot have hung between them.

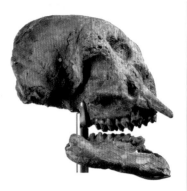

ABOVE Skull of the mastodon *Zygolophodon*, discovered in Greece and dated to 8 million years ago. This skull of a juvenile individual is 40 cm (15¾ in) long and shows an early stage of its tusk growth.

Homo floresiensis; cut-marks on some of the stegodon bones suggest the animals were butchered by, and maybe hunted by, the diminutive people.

The true mastodons

The final major group of proboscideans are the true mastodons. Mastodons are relatively primitive proboscideans, having probably diverged after the *Phiomia* stage but before the gomphotheres (see p.30). The earliest species, *Losodokodon,* is known from fossils found in Kenya, East Africa, some 27–24 million years old. A later form, *Zygolophodon*, spread across Eurasia around 18 million years ago and soon migrated into North America. It was not the ancestor of the 'American mastodon', however. A second wave of immigration brought mastodons of the genus *Mammut* across the Bering land connection around 11 million years ago and from this stock the American mastodon *Mammut americanum* eventually evolved, surviving until only 13,000 years ago. Through this long transition the crushing molars remained relatively unchanged, but the jaws shortened greatly and the lower tusks were lost. The upper tusks, which had started as downwardly directed, became horizontal and finally came to point upward.

RIGHT The tusks of *Mammut borsoni*, a relative of the American mastodon. Excavated in Greece in 2007 and dating to 3 million years ago, they measure around 5 m (16 ft 5 in) in length – the longest tusks of any known creature, living or extinct.

Meanwhile in Europe, the species *Mammut borsoni* evolved, and survived until around 2.5 million years ago. Like the American mastodon, *Mammut borsoni* had a short mandible without lower tusks, implying parallel evolutionary trends from their common ancestor. However, their upper tusks developed to a much greater extent than in their American cousins. In 2007 a partial skeleton of *Mammut borsoni* was unearthed near the town of Milia in northern Greece, in sandy deposits dated to around 3 million years old. The skeleton was identified

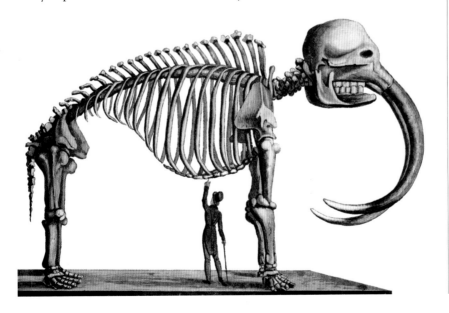

as that of an adult male in its prime, 3.5 m (11½ ft) high at the shoulder and with gently curving tusks. On measuring the left and right tusks they were found to be an astonishing 4.58 and 5.02 m (15 and 16½ ft) long, respectively, along the outer curve. These proved to be the longest tusks ever recorded for any animal living or extinct, earning them a place in the *Guinness World Records*. In total length from the tip of the tusks to the base of the tail the animal measured 8.7 m (28½ ft).

THE AMERICAN MASTODON

The American mastodon and woolly mammoth were quite different animals, but they have been much confused. Both were massive, hairy, elephant-like animals with tusks and trunk, and both lived during the Ice Age, at least in North America. However, in their detailed adaptations and their evolutionary position they were as distinct as a human and a monkey, separated by at least 25 million years of evolution.

Quest for the mastodon

The first reported fossil of the American mastodon was a molar tooth found in 1705 on the banks of the Hudson River in New York State. Further discoveries soon followed, and in 1739 the celebrated Kentucky site of Big Bone Lick came to light where, over many decades, hundreds of mastodon remains were unearthed. The mysterious animal became known as the *Incognitum* ('unknown').

The remains intrigued early American leaders such as Benjamin Franklin and George Washington – the latter had a mastodon molar from Big Bone Lick on his mantelpiece. Thomas Jefferson, when he became President, dispatched an expedition to explore the American West in 1803. Included in its brief was a request to search

BELOW Albert Koch's greatly exaggerated representation of the American mastodon as exhibited in London in 1842, this time with the tusks mounted sideways.

for the *Incognitum*. Jefferson expected the team would discover not only its preserved remains but also the living animals, a hope in which he was to be sorely disappointed.

Eighteenth-century scholars, including Franklin and the British anatomist William Hunter, believed the *Incognitum* to be a terrifying carnivorous creature. They reconstructed the tusks curving downward like two gigantic talons, which they assumed the animal used to capture or hold its prey. When Charles Peale excavated the first complete mastodon skeleton, in New York State in 1801, he mounted it in this dramatic pose. He also publicized it, incorrectly, as the 'skeleton of a mammoth'.

The term 'mammoth' had first been introduced into Europe in the 1690s, and was based on the word 'mammut' or 'mamont' used by Siberian natives to describe the remains found there, which we now know as the woolly mammoth. In 1799, the zoologist G Blumenbach used this term as the basis for a new scientific name *Mammut*, but unfortunately he applied it not to the mammoth but to remains of the American *Incognitum*, stoking the confusion that persists to this day.

As early as 1728, the English scholar Hans Sloane (whose personal collections later formed the core of the British Museum and the Natural History Museum in London) had suggested that the *Incognitum*, the mammoth and the living elephant were different animals, albeit related. This view was finally confirmed by the French anatomist Georges Cuvier in 1796, who demonstrated that the *Incognitum* (i.e. the mastodon) was a herbivorous animal like the living elephants,

LEFT Koch's mastodon skeleton after purchase by the British Museum and re-mounting at its correct size and form. The skeleton is still impressive at around 2.75 m (9 ft) high by 4 m (13 ft ½ in) long excluding the tusks.

ABOVE Excavation of a mastodon skeleton in the town of Hyde Park, New York State, USA, in 2000. Discovered by accident in the back yard of a local resident, the dig uncovered 95% of the skeleton of an adult male some 13,000 years old.

a view which Jefferson, who had previously subscribed to the carnivore theory, immediately accepted.

Mastodons continued to excite public attention. In 1840 an entrepreneur named Albert Koch excavated quantities of mastodon fossils in a river valley in Missouri, USA. He pieced together a skeleton from isolated bones, named it the 'Missouri Levianthan', and took it on tour. The public paid one shilling to marvel at a skeleton which was, in fact, greatly exaggerated in its dimensions, at 5 m (16½ ft) high, 10 m (33 ft) long, and according to Koch's publicity, 7 m (23 ft) between the tips of the tusks! In 1843, after a successful tour of Europe, it went on display in London where Richard Owen, later founder of the Natural History Museum, purchased it on behalf of the British government, paying Koch $2000 plus $1000 a year for life. He re-mounted it at a realistic size and posture, and the skeleton is still to be seen in the Mammal Gallery of the Natural History Museum in London.

Distribution and appearance

Remains of the American mastodon have been found from Alaska to Mexico, and from the Atlantic to the Pacific coasts, but the greatest concentration of remains is in the east and midwest of the USA. Numerous bogs in this region contain bones of single mastodons or of a few individuals. In 1845, farm workers digging a bog in New York State hit something hard – it was the skull of a mastodon. Excavating further, they uncovered a complete skeleton in upright stance, presumably the position in which it had sunk in and died. This was the celebrated 'Warren mastodon', later purchased for US$30,000 by the financier J P Morgan and still on display at the American Museum of Natural History in New York.

The Great Lakes area seems to have been the core of the mastodon's distribution, from which it spread more widely during favourable climatic episodes. In this region mastodon remains are commonly associated with those of other forest animals such as deer and beavers, while in other areas, such as California and Arizona, it is found together with species suggestive of a semi-open, savannah-like habitat.

In height the mastodon was typically 2.7–2.8 m (about 9 ft) at the shoulder, with a body shape that was relatively low and long compared to that of elephants and mammoths. It was a stocky, heavily muscled animal, with a deep chest, wide pelvic region and very robust limbs. The long back was highest at the shoulder and mildly dished behind, lacking the distinctive backward slope of the mammoth. The head was low, wide and with a flat top, contrasting with the domed head of the mammoth. The tusks were up to 2.5 m (over 8 ft) long, upwardly and outwardly curved, again distinct from the mammoth's tusks, which were directed downward from their base and then turned outward and upward. In both body and tusk size, males were somewhat larger than females. In most individuals the lower jaws were tuskless, but some animals bore short lower tusks in addition to the upper pair.

LEFT The 20 cm (8 in) molar tooth of an American mastodon in side view. The low crown and rounded cusps were adapted to crushing the leaves and twigs of mainly coniferous vegetation.

Since there are few mastodon remains preserved in arctic permafrost, we lack the carcasses that have taught us so much about the adaptations of the woolly mammoth. A few pieces of mastodon skin have been found, however, and they bear bundles of fine under-fur interspersed with coarser, hollow guard hairs. The outer hair is 3 to 18 cm (1¼ to 7 in) long and of a dark brown to black colour.

Habitat and adaptations

The plant remains found at mastodon sites in the Great Lakes area mainly reflect coniferous forest including bogs, ponds and marshes. The commonest tree is spruce, followed by pine and larch. Although giving a sense of the mastodon's habitat, it is hard to be sure these species actually represented the animals' diet. Nonetheless, it is generally assumed that mastodons ate the plants that grew around swamps and ponds in their woodland habitat. In a few cases, remains of leaves and twigs found adjacent to mastodon bones are chopped up in a way that suggests they might have been chewed and swallowed by the animal. In the case of the Warren mastodon, crushed twigs and leaves formed a convoluted column about 10 cm (4 in) in diameter and directed through the pelvic orifice; it was assumed to be gut contents reflecting the original shape of the intestine. One mastodon found in New York State had larch twigs still sticking to its teeth.

The association of mastodon remains with formerly boggy areas has led to the interpretation of some of their features as adaptations to wet habitats. One researcher has suggested that the very fine and wavy under-fur, growing in dense bundles, resembles that of the otter and beaver, and could indicate frequent immersion in lakes or ponds. Another has proposed that the unusually thick and heavy limb bones might have helped give the animal ballast while wading through deep water. The mastodon's feet are wide and squat compared to those of elephants and mammoths – a possible adaptation to walking on soft, boggy ground. One modern analogue could be the moose, another inhabitant of coniferous forest, which spends much time immersed in pools feeding on aquatic plants and avoiding insects, and has widely splayed feet for walking on boggy ground.

Mastodon tusks sometimes have flat, polished facets on their side or upper surfaces. These are due to wear in life and suggest that the animals may have been 'shovelling' for food on the ground or in water, or using the tusks for bark-striping trees, as living elephants do. The lower tusks of mastodons, where present, often show similar wear.

An intriguing correlation has been noticed between the size of mastodon remains, their molar form, and the evidence of their former environment. Individuals that lived in spruce-dominated vegetation have smoother, simpler molars but are larger in body size. Those found in pine-dominated habitats have more rugged molars but are smaller in body size. This has led to the tentative suggestion that there were two ecologically adapted forms within the American mastodon, albeit both within the same species, *Mammut americanum*.

ABOVE The end portion of a tusk of American mastodon. This specimen, some 90 cm (35 in) long, shows pronounced flattening on one side of the tip end (catching the light in the photograph), the result of prolonged use during life.

CHAPTER 3
The world of the Ice Age

THE ICE AGE BEGAN AROUND 2.5 MILLION YEARS AGO. The world had been gradually cooling for a much longer period than this – since around 15 million years ago – but at 2.5 million years ago a critical point was reached at which ice-sheets, in effect massive glaciers, began to expand their range across the globe. Today ice-sheets are restricted to areas around the North and South Poles and to small mountain glaciers, but at their maximum extent they extended as far south as southern England, while much of the North American continent was engulfed by an ice-sheet with a total area of some 13 million km² (5 million square miles). The ice, up to 3 km (nearly 2 miles) thick, made major impacts on the landscape over which it rode – carving the rolling upland landscape of much of northern England, for example.

The expansion and contraction of the glaciers happened not once, but multiple times over the past 2.5 million years, each time to a different extent and in slightly

OPPOSITE Two sabre-tooth cats attack a dying mammoth caught in the tar pits of La Brea, California, some 30,000 years ago. One of the cats has become trapped itself, as has a dire wolf in the foreground.

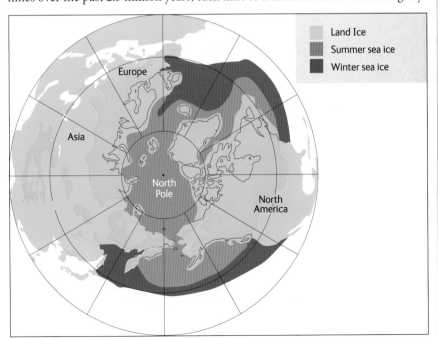

Land Ice
Summer sea ice
Winter sea ice

Europe

Asia

North Pole

North America

LEFT The hugely expanded ice caps of the last glaciation extended to central latitudes of both Europe and North America. As today, sea ice extended even further south during the winter months.

RIGHT A modern glacier in the Andes of Patagonia, Argentina. The growth or contraction of a glacier is a balance between accumulation due to snowfall, and erosion due to melting.

differing directions. This cycle of expansion and contraction was driven, in turn, by cycles of climatic cooling and warming. In one of the most important scientific discoveries of the twentieth century, it was demonstrated in the 1970s that these global climatic cycles are themselves driven by slowly shifting variations in the Earth's spin and in its orbit around the sun, an idea first proposed by the Scotsman James Croll over a hundred years previously.

Ice Age climate change

The most important of these variations is in the shape of the Earth's orbit around the sun, which ranges from an almost perfect circle to a slightly elongated, oval shape. The cycle of change from circle to oval and back again takes around 100,000 years. When in the 'oval' phase, the total amount of solar radiation received by the Earth over the course of a year is reduced, leading to a cooling of climate and expansion of the ice-sheets. In the 'circle' phase radiation increases, climate warms and the glaciers contract. This effect explains why there have been cycles of glaciation every hundred thousand years or so. In between the glacial episodes are

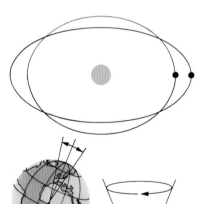

RIGHT The three cyclical variations in the Earth's movement that determine the timing of glaciations. Top: the shape of the orbit around the sun; middle: the tilt of the axis of rotation; bottom: the location of the poles.

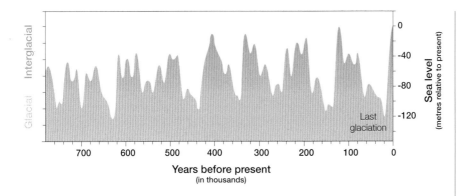

The cycle of glacial and interglacial periods over the past 800,000 years. The present interglacial (warm period) is at the right. Minor climatic fluctuations are superimposed on the main 100,000-year cycle.

much shorter periods of warm climate, known as interglacials, typically 10–15,000 years long. We are currently living in such an interglacial, and previous ones occurred at approximately 100,000, 200,000, 300,000 and 400,000 years ago.

In addition to this effect are two shorter astronomical cycles influencing the Earth's climate. One of them concerns the tilt of the Earth's axis. Currently, the axis of the Earth (the line between the North and South Poles) is tilted at around 23.5 degrees relative to the plane of the Earth's orbit around the sun. However, this angle varies between 22.1 and 24.5 degrees on a repeat cycle of around 41,000 years. As the tilt changes, the distribution of heat between the seasons alters – cool summers during phases of lesser tilt are thought to increase the yearly build-up of snow and ice at high latitudes, leading to expansion of the glaciers. Thirdly, the actual position of the Earth's axis (i.e. the position of the North and South Poles) shifts slightly, on a cycle of around 26,000 years, changing the seasonal contrast. Currently, the Earth is closest to the sun in the northern hemisphere winter, which makes winters there less severe.

These two shorter cycles of climate change, superimposed onto the major 100,000-year cycle, have produced a complicated series of global warming and cooling phases. There are, finally, much shorter climate events, on a scale of a few thousand or even a few hundred years, produced by internal feedback processes within the Earth's climatic system, and producing frequent, sometimes quite violent climatic shifts on top of the slower, astronomically driven cycles. The total effect is that the Earth has been subject to an exceedingly complex and varied series of natural climate changes over the past 2.5 million years. The informal term 'Ice Age' is often used to describe this entire period, as it included many episodes of glacial expansion, even though these were punctuated by milder intervals. Somewhat confusingly, the term is also sometimes applied to the individual glacial episodes, such as the last one, which lasted from about 100,000 to 12,000 years ago. In this book, the expression 'last glaciation' will be used for this interval, and 'Ice Age' reserved for the entirety of the past 2.5 million years. Geologically, that period is known as the Quaternary. The term 'Pleistocene' is also commonly used. It is almost synonymous with the Quaternary but excludes the last 12,000 years – the present interglacial and time of major human impact – which is separated off as the Holocene.

RIGHT Sea level dropped by up to 120 m (393 ft) during glacial periods, exposing a broad area of land between present-day Siberia and Alaska. This allowed migration of many animal species between the continents. Sea ice is shown in white.

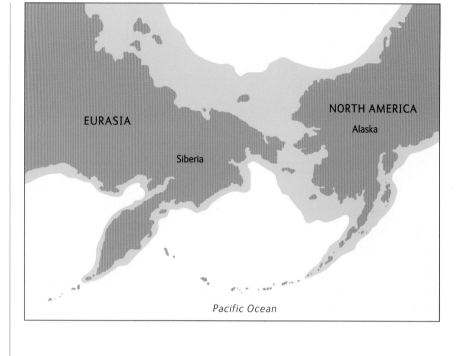

EURASIA

NORTH AMERICA

Alaska

Siberia

Pacific Ocean

BELOW This vertebra (part of the backbone) of a woolly mammoth, dredged from the floor of the North Sea between Britain and Holland, had provided a substrate for barnacles, molluscs and other marine organisms.

LIFE IN THE ICE AGE

Although at their maximum extent the glaciers of the Ice Age covered much more land than they do at present, vast areas of the Earth's surface were untouched by them, and here life continued in abundance. Woolly mammoths and other creatures probably ranged within sight of the glaciers where food was available, but images of mammoths actually walking on ice-sheets, often shown battling against blizzards to eke out a meagre living, are fantastical and false. South of the northern hemisphere glaciers, plant growth was often highly productive, and this supported an abundance of animal life. Even so, the landscapes and habitats were often very different from those of today. These differences resulted not only from changes in the global temperature and seasonal regime, described above, but various 'knock-on' effects that could greatly affect conditions in different regions. In the Tropics, for example, the global cold–warm cycles led to an alternation of wetter and dryer episodes and to shifts in seasonal monsoon patterns. The continuous equatorial belts of rainforest became at times fragmented, and with them their contained animal life, leading to the production of new species as populations became separated. Some desert areas, by contrast, became green as rainfall patterns shifted, allowing the dispersal of grazing species across formerly hostile territory, as described for the spread of early mammoths out of Africa in Chapter 1.

Climatic shifts between glacials and interglacials were profound. In southern England, for example, average temperatures during the last glaciation (100,000–12,000 years ago) were typically around 10°C (50°F) in the summer (6°C or about 11°F colder than today) and –9°C (15.8°F) in the winter (13°C or about 23.5°F colder than today), similar to northern Scandinavia at present. This period of generally cold climate, however, included many minor fluctuations, as explained above. The coldest period occurred between about 25,000 and 20,000 years ago. Known as the 'Last Glacial Maximum', it saw ice-sheets extend as far as central England and winter temperatures plummet to –18°C (0°F) or lower, similar to those of western Siberia today.

Sea-level change

A final major effect of Ice Age climate change, with great implications for animal life, was changes in the level of the world's oceans. With the massive expansion of the glaciers, so much of the world's water was locked up in ice that the sea fell by up to 120 m (nearly 400 ft) relative to today's levels. A broad picture of the effect can be seen by studying any atlas showing current sea depths in different parts of the world. Anywhere with a depth of less than 120 m would potentially have become dry land at some point during the glacial cycle. Areas with much shallower sea depths would have dried out for prolonged periods, sometimes over wide areas. The picture is somewhat complicated by movements of the Earth's crust, which altered the pattern locally, but the overall result was the opening-up of major areas of land surface, and the linking together of regions formally separated by the sea. Among them, a broad land connection, known as Beringia, joined Asia to North America between the regions of present-day northeast Siberia and Alaska; many of the islands of Southeast Asia such as Borneo and the Indonesian archipelago became joined to each other and to the Southeast Asian mainland; New Guinea was joined to Australia; and Britain was broadly joined to the rest of Europe by the exposure of much of the North Sea and English Channel.

The implications for animal life were profound, as species spread their ranges into vast new areas of suitable habitat. On the one hand, this brought previously separated species into contact, leading some to go extinct if they were in competition. On the other hand, populations in newly colonized regions might evolve into new species if they became isolated from their ancestors. The cyclical nature of sea-level change, in keeping with glacial–interglacial cycles, particularly enhanced the latter process, especially when sea level rose again during warm episodes and populations on islands or even different continents found themselves separated. For marine organisms, the same process operated, but precisely out

ABOVE This skull of a young mammoth, dredged from the North Sea, graphically illustrates the effect of sea-level change on the landscape. The skull was not washed into the sea but belonged to an animal that lived there when it was dry land during the last glaciation.

of phase: the Bering land bridge, for example, while creating a passageway for terrestrial animals, isolated the marine faunas of the Pacific and Arctic Oceans.

The evolution and dispersal of mammoths, described in Chapter 1, took place against this backdrop of major global change. The heyday of the final and best-known species, the woolly and Columbian mammoths, was during the last glaciation, broadly between about 100,000 and 12,000 years ago. As the most recent part of the Ice Age, this is also the period for which we have the most detailed information about the creatures that roamed alongside the mammoths, and the habitats in which they lived.

THE WORLD OF THE WOOLLY MAMMOTH

Environment

The range of the woolly mammoth during the last glaciation extended from Norway in the north to Spain in the south, and eastward across the span of the Eurasian continent, encompassing almost all of Europe, Russia and northern China. From there it stretched across Beringia into Alaska and across northern North America to the eastern seaboard. Some of these areas were unpopulated by mammoths at times, thanks to the expansion of glaciers, and the southernmost regions were probably only populated during the coldest episodes. Yet much of this area was inhabited most of the time – a huge geographical range spanning three continents and tens of millions of square kilometres of territory.

From the point of view of large herbivorous mammals such as the woolly mammoth, the key feature of the Ice Age environment was the nature of the vegetation that provided their food. This in turn was largely determined by the climate, but was more important than the climate *per se* in influencing the range and abundance of the mammals. In the current interglacial period, the natural vegetation across the areas formerly inhabited by the woolly mammoth comprises three major zones. In the far north, tundra, a treeless landscape of low-growing plants such as mosses, lichens, sedges and small bushes. South of the tundra, across much of Scandinavia, northern Russia and Canada, coniferous or mixed forest of birch, pine, larch, spruce and other species. Further south again, to Mediterranean latitudes, a variety of landscapes including deciduous forests and large grassy areas known as steppes or prairies.

In the last glaciation, the landscape was very different. Across all of these regions, because of the colder climate, trees were relatively sparse, limited to areas with relatively mild climate where patches of open woodland – mostly of coniferous species – could grow. Elsewhere, across vast areas, a more open vegetation developed, with species in combinations not found anywhere today. This comprised species today living in tundra, such as sedges, mosses and lichen, together with those now characteristic of steppes or prairies, especially various species of grasses. Overall, this vegetation has been described as a cold, dry

grassland. It has also been termed 'steppe–tundra', because it contains a mixture of steppe (grassland) and tundra species, or 'mammoth steppe', after its most famous inhabitant, though in a botanical sense neither of these terms is strictly accurate. Most important, from the point of view of the mammals and other fauna, this vegetation was both varied and productive. 'Productive' in a botanical sense means that plant growth across the year was both substantial and nutritious. Without this, large herds of grazing mammals would not have been able to subsist there. This productivity was aided by a climate which, although too cold for trees, provided a similar daylight regime to today, moderate precipitation, and relatively clear skies giving prolonged exposure to solar radiation for plant growth.

ABOVE Just as the woolly mammoth was a hairy relative of today's elephants, the woolly rhinoceros was a heavily coated relative of the living rhinos. Like the mammoth it subsisted on the cold, grassy plains of the Ice age.

Herbivores

The large mammals coexisting with the woolly mammoth were generally those which, like itself, were adapted to grazing on the open landscape. The largest animal after the mammoth was the woolly rhinoceros. About the size of a living African white rhino, the animal had a body weight of about 2 tonnes, a massive shoulder hump, and a length of around 3.5 m (11½ ft). Although its coat colour is unknown, a high density of hair follicles on the neck of preserved carcasses (see Chapter 4) suggests a thick mane.

The woolly rhino had two horns, each formed from compressed hair like those of all rhinos. The extraordinary front horn was up to 1.2 m (4 ft) long and, unlike that of living rhinos, strongly flattened from side to side, creating a sabre shape. The front edge of the horn often became worn by use into a straight, keeled edge, due to active side-to-side movements of the head, perhaps for snow-clearing to access food beneath. Behind it was a second, shorter horn, typically 60 cm (24 in) long and more rounded in section.

Like today's rhinos, the woolly rhino was probably solitary or lived in small groups. Frozen stomach contents from Siberia show that its diet was usually dominated by low-growing grass, although one carcass contained significant quantities of shrub tundra plants, such as dwarf birch. The skull shape shows that the head hung very low, the animal feeding like a giant 'lawnmower'. In keeping with this, a preserved head from Siberia shows very wide, flat lips, an adaptation to relatively unselective feeding on low vegetation. Although commonly co-occurring with the woolly mammoth, the range of the woolly rhino was not so extensive. It did not penetrate the northernmost regions of Siberia, and never crossed into the New World.

Along with the woolly mammoth and woolly rhino were three species that survive, or at least have close living relatives, today, but which in the last glaciation formed vast herds extending far beyond their modern ranges. These were the

RIGHT The landscape of the last glaciation across northern Eurasia, while largely treeless, produced a rich growth of vegetation that supported large herds of bison, horses and other grazing species.

THE WORLD OF THE ICE AGE

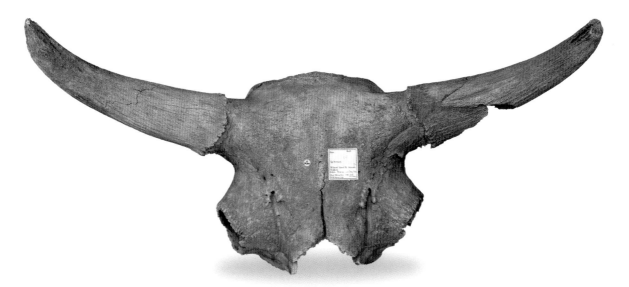

bison, the wild horse, and the reindeer or caribou. The bison of the Ice Age, sometimes known as the steppe bison, was closely related to the living bison (buffalo) of North America, but extended in the Ice Age across northern Asia and Europe as well. It was a little larger than living bison, males weighing up to a tonne with a body length of 3 m (10 ft), females somewhat smaller. Cave art from France and Spain shows an animal with very powerful front quarters and a high shoulder hump, up to 2 m (6½ ft) from the ground. The horns were also proportionately larger than in living bison, with a spread of nearly a metre between the tips in large males. Frozen remains from Alaska show that the horns were black in colour, while the coat was in general a rich brown, with dark brown to blackish areas on

ABOVE The horns and skull roof of an Ice Age bison, found in gravels of the River Thames west of London. With a horn span of 75 cm (29½ in), the remains are around 80,000 years old, soon after the start of the last glaciation.

ABOVE Vast herds of wild reindeer or caribou, a species today limited to the far north, ranged southwards across much of Europe and North America during the last glaciation.

the limbs. Plant remains wedged into the molar teeth of fossil bison from Alaska reveal a high predominance of grass food, but a small amount of herbs, bark and moss too. Males and females may have formed separate herds, though herd sizes were probably not as large as historically seen in American plains bison – maybe in the dozens rather than hundreds.

The wild horse was equally widespread in the last glaciation, occupying most of northern Eurasia and North America. Horses survive today as the huge variety of 'artificially' created domestic breeds, but the endangered Przewalski's horse of Mongolia, the only surviving truly 'wild' horse, is clearly little-changed from its Ice Age ancestors. Horses depicted in cave art are strikingly similar in, for example, the compact body, upright mane, and white nose tip. Horses, with their extremely high-crowned cheek teeth, are grazing animals *par excellence*, and must have been particularly abundant in the more grassy regions of Ice Age Eurasia.

Reindeer today live in Scandinavia and northern Siberia, as well as Alaska and northern Canada where they are known as caribou. In the last glaciation, however, their range extended as far south as northern Spain. They are the only species of deer in which the females, as well as the males, carry antlers. The species today forms vast herds, some of which undertake seasonal migrations of hundreds of kilometres, and the same was probably true in the last glaciation, to judge from the massive quantities of fossil remains found in Europe. The modern species shows many adaptations that would have served it well under Ice Age conditions. These include anti-freeze substances in the feet to prevent the freezing-up of lubricating oils, and wide, curved hooves allowing it to walk on top of crusty snow. The feeding adaptation of reindeer is, however, very different from that of the bison or horse. With low-crowned teeth, it was not adapted to the tough grasses of the open steppes, but to lichens, mosses and sedges.

Two other hoofed mammals strikingly reflect the 'mixed' nature of the habitat shown by the vegetation. These are the musk-ox and the saiga antelope, species that coexisted at times during the last glaciation, whereas today their ranges are widely separated. The spread of musk-oxen into central Europe, even more than that of reindeer, graphically conveys the climatic regime of the times, as it is today confined to the high Arctic of Canada and Greenland. Its fossil remains in Europe are not common, suggesting that it only ventured this far

BELOW This skull of a musk-ox, preserved in permafrost since the last glaciation, retains not only the bony structures but also the outer keratin sheath of the horns. Measuring 50 cm (20 in) across, it was found on the Seward Peninsula of Alaska.

south during the more extreme climatic episodes. Today's musk-oxen have the longest, thickest winter coat of any animal, called qiviut and with eight times more insulating capacity than sheep's wool. Living in small herds, it is a tundra animal, but its range is restricted to relatively snow-free areas, as unlike the reindeer it is not adept at digging food out from under the snow.

LEFT At up to 3.5 m (11 ft 6 in) in span and made of solid bone, the giant deer's antlers were the largest of any known species, living or extinct. The antlers were shed and regrown each year.

ABOVE Spotted hyaenas, accompanied by a wake of vultures, scavenge an elephant carcass in modern-day Africa. In Ice Age Europe spotted hyaenas scavenged, and occasionally hunted, woolly mammoths.

In contrast to the musk-ox, the saiga antelope is today a grazing animal of the steppe, the grassy plains of central Asia far to the south of the modern tundra. Saiga are smallish animals typically 70 cm (28 in) high and weighing around 50 kg (110 lb), the males bearing short horns. The saiga is notable for its large, flexible nose structure, serving to conserve moisture in its dry environment and which would have served to warm the inspired air in glacial climates.

Other species of a more temperate climatic and habitat tolerance coexisted with the woolly mammoth in the more southerly areas of its huge range. Perhaps the most celebrated was the giant deer, also known as the 'Irish elk' because its remains are abundant in Ireland, although its range extended across Europe to central Asia. Giant deer reached around 1.8 m (6 ft) at the shoulder and weighed around 500 kg (1,100 lb). Cave art indicates a strong back hump over the shoulder, dark in colour compared to the lighter coat overall, and what appears to be a ring around the neck and one or two diagonal lines down the body.

The fame of this animal rests on its spectacular antlers, borne by the males only. They grew in size and complexity through the animal's youth, reaching a span of 2.5 to 3.5 m (8 to 11½ ft) in adult stags. Shed each year in the spring, they were grown through the summer, and used in fighting during late autumn and winter. Research on the microscopic structure of the antler bone shows marked strengthening along the front edge, indicating use in fighting, not just in display as some had believed, although the size and symmetry of the antlers also had a likely influence on females' choice of a mate. The antlers are shown off to their maximum extent when the head is held aloft (i.e. looking straight forward). This may have been enough, combined with bellowing, to disarm a rival. If it came to a fight, the heads would have been lowered, bringing the long points to the fore for interlocking with, and ultimately goring, the opponent.

The giant deer lived in small herds and was not an abundant species, perhaps because the mineral requirements of the huge antlers restricted it to areas of particularly rich vegetation. It was an animal of flat plains and light relief, frequenting lightly wooded areas, or semi-open grass and shrub vegetation with scattered copses of trees, and subsisting on a mixed diet of grass and soft leaves.

Carnivores

The diversity and abundance of herbivorous mammals in the Ice Age supported an array of carnivorous species. Their presence is recognized not only from their fossil remains but also from traces of their activity, such as fossilized droppings, and gnaw marks on preserved bones of their prey.

One such species was the spotted hyaena which, with a range extending from Africa into Europe, southern Siberia and China, was far more widely distributed in the Ice Age than today. Similar to the modern species, the fossil form differed mainly in its somewhat larger body size. The animals frequently inhabited caves, indicated by the abundance of their bones and teeth, including those of juveniles, at many cave sites. The fossil deposits also frequently contain remains of their prey

ABOVE The end of a woolly mammoth limb-bone bearing chewing marks of spotted hyaena. The specimen is from Kent's Cavern, southwest England, used as a den by hyaenas during the last glaciation.

BELOW A selection of the woolly mammoth teeth found at Kent's Cavern, together with a mandible of spotted hyaena. The teeth, 5–10 cm (2–4 in) long, are all of juvenile mammoths, suggesting a size limit to the hunting capacity of the hyaenas.

RIGHT The cave bear was related to the living brown and grizzly bears but is classified as a separate species. Many of the remains found in caves are of animals that died during hibernation.

– usually splinters of bone covered with chew-marks – as well as preserved hyaena droppings. These hard, white, spherical objects are the size of a walnut, and survive because they are rich in phosphate, a legacy of the hyaenas' taste for chewing up bone. Like their modern counterparts, the hyaenas hunted in packs, and also scavenged carcasses. One cave in southern England, Kent's Cavern, contained hundreds of hyaena bones and droppings, and among their prey remains are large numbers of woolly mammoth teeth, almost all of them from mammoths under 3 years of age. Such animals, already about a tonne in body weight, reflect the size limit which the hyaenas could hunt, or whose jointed carcasses they could drag back to their lair.

The lion was even more widely distributed in the Ice Age than the spotted hyaena, with a broad range extending across Europe, Siberia and North America. Although they were closely related to the living species *Panthera leo*, recent DNA evidence indicates that the Ice Age lions of Europe and northern Asia were sufficiently distinct to be regarded as a separate species, *Panthera spelaea*. The bones from these regions show an animal somewhat larger than the modern African

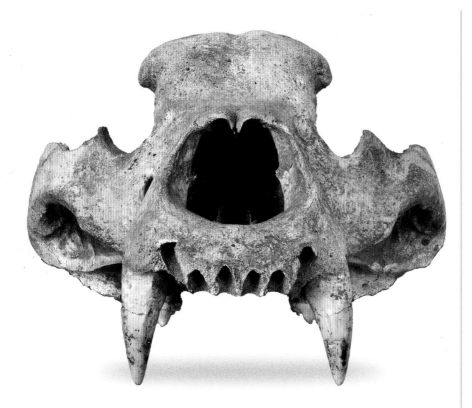

LEFT The skull of a cave bear from a cave in Hungary, seen from the front. Although a vegetarian, it sported massive canine teeth to ward off enemies. In this specimen the incisor teeth inbetween have been lost.

lion, and images from cave art suggest that males lacked a mane. They took mainly medium-sized mammalian prey, up to the size of a bison, as graphically shown by bite-marks in the skull of a fully grown bison found in Alaska. Recent isotope studies of preserved lion bones confirm that bison were particularly favoured by lions in the last glaciation.

The cave bear is now extinct, and even in the last glaciation had a limited distribution, with almost all of its remains found in central and southern regions of Europe. A bear of very large size – larger than the American grizzly – it was marked out by a pronounced 'step' shape of the forehead, clearly seen in preserved skulls. The name 'cave bear' is apt: some caves in central and eastern Europe have yielded vast quantities of remains – up to 30,000 individuals in one Austrian cave alone. There is also graphic evidence of its activity in caves such as Rouffignac in southern France, where a series of shallow hollows on the floor evidently represent nests made by cave bears for their winter hibernation. The cave walls are covered by claw marks, presumably left as the animals felt their way in the pitch blackness. While most species of bear consume both meat and vegetable matter, chemical studies of fossil bones confirm what had been suspected from its teeth – that the cave bear was almost exclusively a vegetarian.

Other carnivores inhabiting the woolly mammoth's terrain included the wolf, brown bear, wolverine, and arctic fox – all species familiar from today's northern fauna, but of greater geographical extent in the last glaciation.

RIGHT A living packrat (*Neotoma*) carrying items to build its nest. A single nest can accumulate layers over hundreds of generations of the rodent, leaving a valuable record of past vegetation and climate.

THE WORLD OF THE COLUMBIAN MAMMOTH

Environment

The range of the Columbian mammoth during the last glaciation covered most of the North American continent south of the great ice-sheet. In modern terms this corresponds to the continental USA (excepting the northeast) and Mexico. The difference between the habitats occupied by the Columbian mammoth and those of its woolly cousin are mainly due to the Columbian mammoth living further to the south. Its distribution was the equivalent, in the Old World, of a range from southern France to North Africa. It was therefore largely south of the 'steppe–tundra' zone inhabited by the woolly mammoth.

An unusual line of evidence of past environments in North America has been provided by a species of rodent called a packrat. Packrats build large nests by accumulating sticks and other items, and anointing them with urine. This contains a sticky, sugary substance that not only cements the nest together but preserves it, sometimes for thousands of years. Packrat nests excavated in caves have provided a treasure-chest of information, since they contain identifiable plant remains dating back up to 50,000 years into the last glaciation. They show that the Ice Age vegetation of the USA and Mexico comprised a varying mosaic of grassland, parkland (a mixed landscape of trees and grassy areas), and open woodlands of various kinds. This variety of habitats, as well as adjacent ones probably less frequented by the mammoths such as scrublands and swamps, supported a greater diversity of large mammals than in the woolly mammoth's range. Some of the more remarkable species will be described here.

Herbivores

Some of the herbivore types living alongside the Columbian mammoth were familiar from more northern areas – horses and bison, for example – but formed distinct species. Up to 10 horse species have been named, based on differences in fossil bones and teeth, and while this may be an exaggeration, there were certainly different kinds – from the 'giant horse' weighing up to half a tonne, to the small 'Mexican horse' that also ranged across the western USA. The bison of the southern plains was related to the northern species but much more imposing, with a body weight of 1.5 tonnes and huge, outstretched horns over 2 m (6½ ft) in total span.

Other bizarre horned mammals included extinct species of musk-ox related to those of the far north but adapted to a completely different, woodland habitat. In one species, the males bore horns that were flattened at their base and fused across the animal's forehead to withstand the force of running clashes as the animals fought. Among various species of deer was the extinct stag-moose, a relative of the living moose but with antlers spreading horizontally from the head in three sections, forming a flamboyant three-dimensional structure.

It may be surprising that camels and llamas were elements of the Ice Age fauna of North America. Now living, respectively, in Asia and South America, these groups originated in North America and survived into the last glaciation where they lived alongside the Columbian mammoth. The commonest species, the charmingly named Yesterday's camel, was like a long-legged version of the living

ABOVE The huge bison of the Ice Age plains and woodlands of southern North America (*Bison latifrons*) had horns up to two metres in span. They were used to establish dominance in fights, and also to ward off predators.

RIGHT Yesterday's camel, *Camelops hesternus*, was one of the last of many species of camel that had inhabited North America. Living mainly in the central and western USA, it was a herbivore eating a broad spectrum of plant types.

RIGHT One of several species of giant sloth in Ice Age North America, the Shasta ground sloth (*Nothrotheriops*) had sharp claws that were probably used for digging and for defence against predators such as *Smilodon*.

Asian dromedary (one-humped) camel but with even thicker lips, and probably lived in large herds. The group also produced a giant, the Nebraska camel, which reached shoulder heights of 3.5 m or 11½ ft (the same as a female mammoth) and weighed a tonne. It became extinct around a million years ago – well before the last glaciation – but coexisted with early Columbian mammoths.

More remarkable still were the bizarre mammals that had arisen in South America during its long isolation as an 'island continent'. When the Panama isthmus began to form about 3 million years ago, some of these mammals migrated north. Around eight different species of sloth lived in North America during the Ice Age. While living sloths are relatively small, slow-moving mammals that hang upside-down from trees, the Ice Age sloths were much larger, flat-footed, ground-living creatures. The species varied in size, but all had heavily built skeletons with powerful limbs and claws, and relatively small heads. A large, weighty tail allowed them to rear up and browse on tall trees, the tail and massive hind limbs forming a supporting 'tripod'. At the small end of the range, the Shasta ground sloth weighed in at around 150 kg (330 lb) and must have been a peculiar animal to behold, its small head perched on a relatively long neck, ambling along on its knuckles to browse shrub vegetation. In dry caves in the southwest USA, skeletons

BELOW The 3 m (10 ft) long skeleton of a glyptodont, a slow-moving mammal, relying for defence on its rigid shell of bony plates. Unlike turtles, it could not withdraw its head into the shell, so protected it with a bony cap.

of this species have been found together with remains of its spiral-shaped dung and coarse yellow hair, still preserved after some 13,000 years. Analysis of the dung reveals a predominance of thorn bushes and other semi-desert vegetation in its diet. At the other end of the scale, *Eremotherium* was related to the giant *Megatherium* of South America but lived in the southern USA. At 6 m (nearly 20 ft) in length and weighing up to 4 tonnes – as much as an elephant – it could reach high into trees in upright posture, and recent research on the mechanics of its skeleton suggests it walked upright on its hind legs as well as ambling on all fours like other ground sloths.

The other 'bizarre' group of South American immigrants were the glyptodonts, giant relatives of the living armadillos. These have been called the tanks of the mammal world, or, in the case of the largest species from South America, likened to a Volkswagen Beetle car. Three species lived in North America, the largest, *Glyptotherium*, measuring 3 m (10 ft) long and weighing around a tonne. Its body was enclosed in a rigid shell or carapace made of up to 2,000 polygonal bony 'tiles'. The tail was also covered in bony plates but jointed, allowing it to move from side to side as the animal waddled along. The tail may also have been used as a side-swiping weapon: calculations suggest that it packed enough energy to fracture the shell of another glyptodont, and the damage observed on some fossil carapaces has been interpreted as the result of fighting. On top of the animal's head was a further protective plate, recalling the armour of a mediaeval knight. Glyptodonts in North America were restricted to the southern part of the continent where they inhabited areas of sub-tropical vegetation on which they browsed.

BELOW Compared to a modern grey wolf, the dire wolf had shorter, sturdier limbs and a 30% more powerful bite. It hunted in packs, allowing it to bring down large-bodied prey.

A final large herbivore coexisting with the Columbian mammoth was its distant cousin the mastodon, whose biology has been described in Chapter 2. Although the areas inhabited by the two giants were largely distinct, it is very likely that they encountered each other in some areas, such as on the edges of open woodlands where their habitats met.

Carnivores

The large carnivores preying on this abundance of animal protein included many species unique to the North American continent, although they were related to species of Europe and Asia. The dire wolf was the size of a modern wolf but more heavily built, with powerful teeth and jaws. Over 1,600 individuals have been found perfectly preserved in the tar pits of La Brea in California, where they

BELOW Skull of *Smilodon*, the most celebrated of Ice Age predators. To enable use of the dramatically elongated canines, the animal also had an enormously wide gape – up to 130° at full stretch, compared to 65° in living big cats.

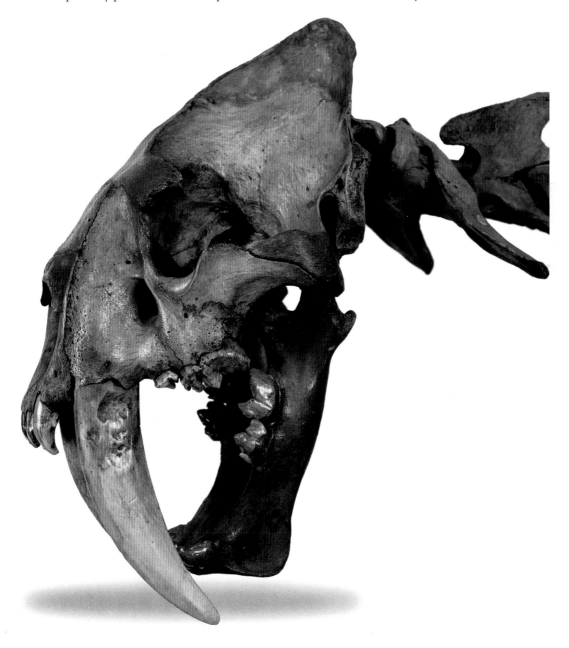

came to feast on animals stuck in the tar but presumably got stuck and perished themselves. Another extinct species was the American lion, whose relationships were uncertain until researchers recently isolated DNA from their preserved bones and showed that they were related to the Eurasian cave lion (see above), descending from a population of the latter which must have crossed the Bering Strait some 300,000 years ago.

There were a number of species of sabre-tooth cats in Ice Age North America, not all of them closely related to each other. One of them, the scimitar cat, was larger than an African lion, and with longer legs and neck. Its canines were 10 cm (4 in) long, strongly flattened side to side, and with a serrated cutting edge that has been likened to a steak knife. Calculations suggest it was capable of short bursts of speed up to 65 km per hour (40 mph). At one remarkable cave in Texas, excavators found the intact remains of at least 13 cubs and 20 adults – the animals were evidently denning in the cave. Alongside them were the remains of more than 200 juvenile mammoths, mostly under 2 years of age when they died. Like the hyaenas from Kent's Cavern in England (see above), the cats were apparently targeting young mammoths, in this case Columbians, which were both vulnerable and manageable.

BELOW The short-faced bear was a giant – probably the largest carnivorous mammal ever to live in North America. Its habits are something of a mystery, however – although long-legged, it lacked the agility to be a rapid pursuit predator.

The most celebrated of the sabre-tooth cats was *Smilodon*. About the size of a modern lion or tiger but more heavily built, it weighed around three-quarters of a tonne and sported massive, curved canines projecting up to 17 cm (7 in) below the upper lip. Its bulk and relatively short legs suggest it was an ambush predator, pouncing on prey such as ground sloths and bison. Recent research suggests that the old idea of sabre-tooth cats using their canines to slash at or bring down moving prey are implausible, since there would have been high risk of breakage to the long and slender canines. Instead, the prey was probably brought down by the cat's powerful front limbs, and only once the prey was immobile would the canines have been pressed into the flesh of the belly or neck, cutting nerves and blood vessels and creating gashing wounds from which the animal would have bled to death.

Among several bear species was a giant – the short-faced bear which, as its name implies, had a wide face and short snout, giving its face a flattened appearance almost like that of a cat. An inhabitant of grasslands in the west of the continent, the short-faced bear was long-legged and, at up to 3 m (10 ft) high when rearing onto its hind legs, would have dwarfed any living bear. It had powerful jaws and teeth and is believed to have had a largely carnivorous diet, an idea supported by chemical analyses of its bones. How much of its food was obtained by hunting and how much by scavenging is, however, an open question.

The large-mammal faunas of the Eurasian and North American continents during the last glaciation were both abundant and remarkably diverse – in distinct contrast to today's relatively impoverished world. Moreover, many of the species described above were linked ecologically to the two mammoth species and the mastodon – whether as predators or as competitors for food and space. The changing climates and habitats of the Ice Age provide the essential backdrop to understanding the adaptations and lifestyles of all these species, as well as the reasons for their extinction.

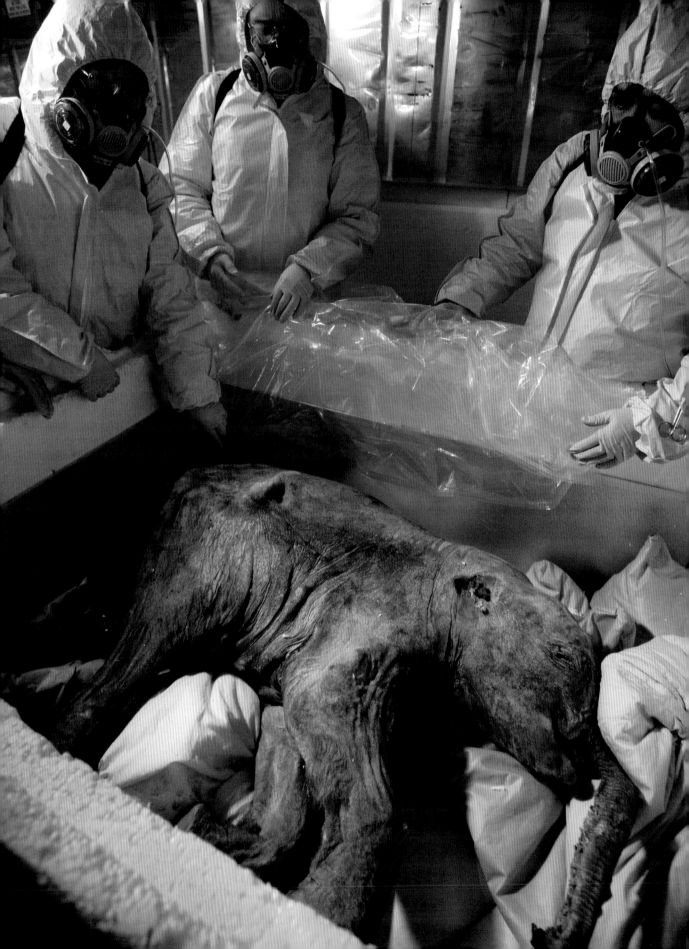

CHAPTER 4
Frozen and living

WE KNOW MORE ABOUT THE APPEARANCE AND NATURAL HISTORY of the woolly mammoth than for any other extinct prehistoric animal. This is mainly because, for the mammoth and a few other Ice Age species, we have the unique advantage of complete carcasses preserved in the frozen soils of the Arctic. For almost all other fossil species we have only preserved teeth and bones to reconstruct the living creature.

Native peoples of the Arctic have been finding frozen carcasses of mammoths and other beasts for centuries. Often they were considered to be giant animals that lived, mole-like, underground, and died on exposure to light, neatly explaining why no-one ever saw one alive. Beginning in the eighteenth century, some of the finds were retrieved for scientific study, though only a dozen or so complete or largely complete mammoth carcasses have been recovered to date. The rate of discovery is increasing, however, due partly to the accelerated thawing of the frozen ground (permafrost) in which they lie buried – one of the few beneficial effects of global

OPPOSITE **The baby mammoth Lyuba, found in Siberia in 2006, is the most complete frozen mammoth carcass ever discovered. It has produced a wealth of information about the mammoth's anatomy and adaptations.**

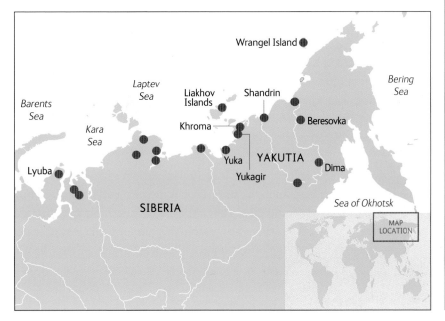

LEFT Localities in northern Siberia where some key frozen carcasses and other mammoth remains have been found. Named sites are those mentioned in the text.

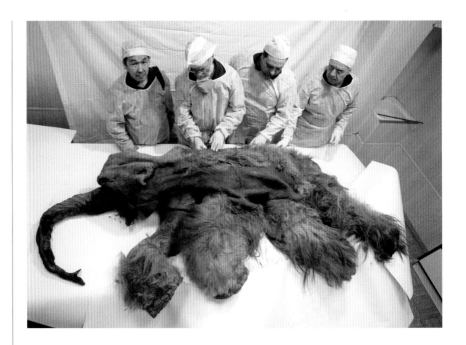

warming. In 2002 the perfectly preserved head of an adult individual, together with a leg, was uncovered in the Yukagir region of northeast Siberia. This was followed in 2006/07 by the sensational discovery of the baby carcass 'Lyuba' (see below). In 2008, another largely complete but more degraded baby carcass was found, named 'Khroma' after its place of discovery close to the Arctic Ocean in Yakutia. And in 2009 an older juvenile was recovered from the arctic shore of the Taimyr peninsula a little to the west; this individual, nicknamed 'Yuka', is around 2 m (6½ ft) long and estimated to have been two and a half years old at death.

Of these, the baby mammoth Lyuba is the most intact mammoth carcass ever discovered, and has been subject to the most intensive scientific research, considerably expanding our knowledge of the woolly mammoth's appearance and way of life. Daniel Fisher, who has led much of the research, recalls his astonishment, on first seeing her, that even her eyelashes were preserved – after some 45,000 years of burial.

Lyuba was found on the banks of the Yuribei River, north of the Arctic Circle in a region of Siberia known as the Yamal peninsula. Although first spotted in September 2006, she was recovered only in May of the following year, thanks to the actions of a local reindeer herdsman whose 10-year old son had first alerted him to the strange carcass exposed in the snow. Lyuba's situation was unusual: resting on the surface of the river bank without any enclosing sediment. Almost certainly, she had travelled down-river before being washed up on the bank. Every year in this region, the spring melting of snow and ice leads to erosion of river banks, often with the dramatic collapse of large blocks of permafrost sediment. Lyuba was probably encased within such a block, which would have rapidly melted in the water, releasing her body into the stream.

LEFT Lyuba's burial and preservation. Left: After death, Lyuba sinks into wet clay and silt. Centre: The ground turns to permafrost, freezing and dehydrating the carcass. Right: In 2006 a block containing Lyuba is washed into the river. It disintegrates and her body is deposited on a sandbar.

Lyuba's body has been subject to a battery of scientific tests, including magnetic resonance imaging (MRI) and computerized tomography (CT) scanning, endoscopy, autopsy, chemical analysis and microscopic examination of tissues. These have been used, firstly, to build up a picture of how she died and was buried. Secondly, they tell us about her individual life and that of woolly mammoths in general.

BELOW Reconstruction of Lyuba in life. The relatively large head, but low head dome and shoulder hump, are typical of young animals.

LYUBA'S DEATH AND PRESERVATION

An initial suggestion for Lyuba's demise was that she had drowned. The large intestine was found to contain food remains (see below), but also fragments of organisms that must have originated in a lake or stream. These included remains of freshwater plants (diatoms and algae), needle-like spikes that form the skeletons of freshwater sponges, and even egg-cases of water-fleas. Subsequent examination of the stomach and small intestine revealed no remains of this kind, however, making drowning less likely

and leading to the suggestion that the aquatic remains were ingested, ultimately from drinking water, while Lyuba was still alive.

A further observation, visible on the CT scans, was that the two elongated nostrils running down the trunk were plugged with fine sediment. The fine, clay-like particles had also penetrated the windpipe, but had not extended into the lungs themselves, which had completely collapsed. Drowning (in water) would produce only a small amount of particulate matter in the respiratory system, and it would have dispersed right into the lungs. The clogging of the trunk and windpipe leads to an alternative scenario: Lyuba suffocated after inhaling viscous sediment, probably after falling into deep mud. This could also explain why the breathing tubes at the base of the trunk had collapsed, leading to the marked depression seen on the front of her face (see p.79): it was a last attempt to breathe in while the trunk was blocked.

After death the carcass must have been quickly buried in the soft sediment, for it shows no sign of attack by predatory mammals or birds. The low-oxygen conditions of the dense sediment also limited bacterial decay. The loss of hair over most of Lyuba's body is not unexpected, since slippage of hair follicles from carcasses under wet conditions is normal within days of death.

Other frozen mammoths

Not all frozen mammoths died in the same way, however. The first baby mammoth discovered, the individual known as Dima, excavated in 1977, had lost all his body fat, and his digestive system contained no food but silt and fragments of hair. It is suggested that he too had become trapped in thick mud but, unlike Lyuba, had

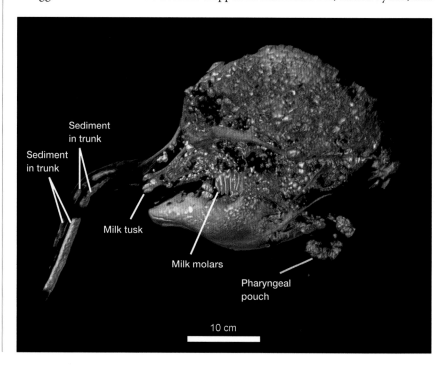

RIGHT CT scan of Lyuba's head. To the left, sediment infilling of the nostrils in the trunk. The milk tusk and molars are also visible. Below and to the right, the pharyngeal pouch is picked out by sediment infilling.

Sediment
in trunk

Sediment
in trunk

Milk tusk

Milk molars

Pharyngeal
pouch

10 cm

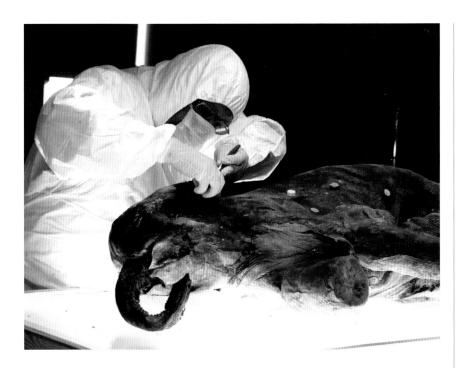

LEFT Lyuba's autopsy. The skin of the head is being carefully pulled away on the left side, allowing extraction of the teeth.

remained alive for a long time, imbibing silt and pulling at his own hair before finally dying of hunger and exhaustion and sinking into the sediment. The case of the celebrated Beresovka carcass – an adult male recovered in 1901 and still on display in the Zoology Museum of St Petersburg – was different again: the animal still had a half-chewed wad of food between its teeth, and several of its bones were broken. It had seemingly fallen suddenly into a deep crevasse and died instantly, soon being covered by the mobile soil that flows over the surface in the Arctic during the brief summer thaw. At depth, the soil would have quickly re-frozen and remained in that state, preserving the enclosed carcass, until finally eroded and rediscovered. In yet another scenario, the carcass found on the Khatanga River, Siberia in 1977 was enclosed in sediments of a kind deposited on the banks of flowing rivers. The animal had evidently lain in the open after death before being covered in sediment; this was consistent with the more decayed state of the carcass, with exposed bones and flesh preserved only in parts.

Lyuba's tissues, although very well preserved, were hard and dry, especially on the outside, and her body was somewhat flattened, but not only through compression. Like other frozen carcasses, she had become mummified – an apt term as it implies preservation by complete drying out. In the case of the deliberately preserved mummies from ancient Egypt, drying was achieved by chemical means such as salting. In the naturally mummified animal carcasses from the permafrost, moisture within the flesh had gradually separated out, forming crystallized ice in the sediment around the carcass. In the process the flesh had gradually dried and shrunk to a greater or lesser degree. As a result, Lyuba weighed 50 kg (110 lb) on discovery – around half her likely live weight.

RIGHT Hair of an adult mammoth. Left, the coarse outer guard hairs, 60 cm (24 in) long. Right, at larger scale, a tuft of inner hair, showing at the top the finest underwool close to the skin, and below, 10-cm (4-in) long hair of intermediate thickness. The orange colour is probably artificial.

 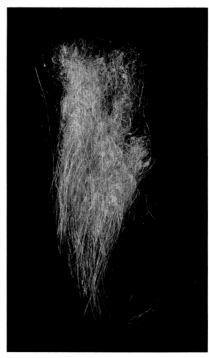

RIGHT Hair of an adult mammoth. Left, the coarse outer guard hairs, 60 cm (24 in) long. Right, at larger scale, a tuft of inner hair, showing at the top the finest underwool close to the skin, and below, 10-cm (4-in) long hair of intermediate thickness. The orange colour is probably artificial.

BELOW This cube of fat, cut from the back of a frozen mammoth carcass, retains its greasy feel. The fat lay beneath the skin and is around 2 cm (1 in) thick.

THE NATURAL HISTORY OF A MAMMOTH

Lyuba's autopsy revealed that as well as her perfectly preserved external anatomy, most of her organs were also present: the heart, lungs, stomach, intestines and liver could all be seen, and further studies have greatly increased our understanding of mammoth biology.

In the first place, Lyuba could be immediately identified as a female from her external genitalia, which closely resembled those of a female elephant. In addition, although only a baby, she showed two nipples, on her underside between her front legs. This is the first time that nipples have been identified in mammoths, and they mirror those in living elephants, which are unusual among mammals in their forward position. Conversely, Lyuba shows no sign of the opening for a musth gland, a characteristic of males among today's elephants. This gland is located in the side of the face, where it produces a pungent, sticky secretion that runs down the bull's face once a year when he is sexually active and said to be 'in musth'. In the perfectly preserved head of the Yukagir male found in 2002, the presence of a musth gland was observed for the first time in a mammoth, in the form of its characteristic opening on the face. This suggested that mammoths experienced musth like living elephants, the secretion presumably being soaked up by the facial fur which distributed its scent onto the breeze.

Protection from the cold

Only patches of hair remain on Lyuba's carcass, but they show the dense fur and orangey colour seen on other carcasses and sometimes found loose as tufts adjacent to preserved skeletons. In an adult the long outer hairs of the coat were up to 1 m (3 ft) long, each strand 0.25–0.5 mm ($\frac{1}{100}$ to $\frac{1}{50}$ in) in diameter – four to six times thicker than human hair. Underneath this shaggy coat was a layer of shorter and finer hair, and next to the skin an insulating underwool. In the recently discovered juvenile called 'Yuka', the hair is a pale yellowish colour with hints of orange (see p.74), leading to its description in the media as 'strawberry blond'. It is unclear to what extent this lack of pigment or the orange colour is natural, or the result of changes through long burial. In a carcass found on Liakhov Island in the Arctic Ocean in 1903 and preserved in the National Museum of Natural History in Paris, the fur is dark brown throughout. Is this the natural colour of all mammoths, or did they vary in their appearance? Remarkable new evidence on this question has come from studies of DNA, described below.

Fur was not the only way mammoths were protected from the cold. Under her skin Lyuba had a layer of white fat ranging from 1 to 4 cm (around ½ to 1½ in) in thickness. This served not only for insulation but also as energy storage, and

BELOW The baby mammoth Lyuba. A month old when she died, the total length of her body is 1.2 m (3 ft 11 in). Typical mammoth features including the very small ear and tail, and flattened sides to the trunk, are clearly visible.

ABOVE Lyuba's trunk tip, seen from behind. The long front 'finger', and shorter back 'thumb' (pointing out of the page) were adapted for picking low-growing plants.

makes clear that Lyuba was well fed and probably in good health at the time of her death.

A further mass of fat was found on the back of Lyuba's neck. Visible from the outside as a hemispherical bulge, autopsy revealed it to be composed of an oily yellowish substance. Under the microscope its tissue structure was similar to that of brown fat – a specialized tissue whose function in mammals is to keep the animal warm by re-heating the blood returning from the surface of the body. This could have been vital for the survival of a young mammoth born in the chilly temperatures of early spring in the high Arctic.

Adaptations to the arctic climate are also seen in the external anatomy. Lyuba has tiny ears and an extremely short tail – confirming observations on the baby mammoth Dima from 1977. Nor was this simply a feature of juvenile animals that had not completed growth, as it is seen also in adults, such as the Yukagir carcass mentioned above, and the celebrated Beresovka mammoth from 1901. In living elephants, by contrast, the ears are very large and the tail hangs well below the knee. The difference in ear size is unlikely to be related to their social function, since large ears would have made excellent signalling devices in the open landscapes inhabited by the mammoth. Instead, the small ears and tail are both likely to have been adaptations for reducing heat loss, and even avoiding frostbite, in exposed organs in an arctic climate. Living elephants are tropical animals with the opposite problem of overheating, and they flap their ears, which are full of blood vessels, in an attempt to cool down.

The mammoths's trunk and tusks

As mentioned above, Lyuba's bronchial passages were filled with fine sediment, visible as dense areas on the CT scans. This led to a remarkable discovery: a patch of sediment in the area between the back of the tongue and the larynx picks out the pharyngeal pouch – the first time this structure has been identified in a mammoth. Its dual function was only confirmed in living elephants as recently as 1998. Adjacent to the larynx, it is used partly in communication, forming a resonating chamber for sounds produced by the vocal chords. Additionally, it can store several litres of water. Elephants drink by sucking up water into the two tubes (nostrils) that run the length of the trunk. The water is not sucked through to the mouth as though with a drinking-straw; instead the full trunk is lifted and inserted into the mouth until its tip is at the top of the oesophagus – and also just above the opening to the pharyngeal pouch. The water is then squirted out – much of it swallowed, but some of it stored in the pouch. Desert elephants in Namibia have been observed spraying themselves with water they had imbibed several hours previously, retrieved by placing the trunk in the mouth and sucking up the water stored in the pharyngeal pouch. Mammoths, it seems, could perform the same trick.

Lyuba's trunk is itself the most perfectly preserved known from a frozen carcass, and has confirmed some specialized features unique to mammoths. At its tip are two protrusions, similar to those of an Asian elephant, but with the front one much longer than in the living species, so that the two form a 'finger and thumb' that would have been served by strong muscles and capable of plucking the low-growing plants that formed the bulk of the mammoth's food. In living elephants the trunk as a whole is formed from up to 100,000 separately moveable parts of muscles, and in mammoths this would have been similar, so it doubtless also used the trunk to wrap around and pull up clumps of longer grasses and other vegetation. Most remarkable in Lyuba, however, is the presence of two flanges of skin forming elongated 'wings' on either side of the trunk. Their presence had been previously suspected from only one specimen: the tip of a trunk hacked from a carcass in 1924 and preserved in the Zoology Museum of St Petersburg. It shows similar flanges, but as it is only one specimen, and very incomplete, it was uncertain if this was a general feature of the woolly mammoth. Lyuba's trunk indicates that this was indeed the case. The function of the flanges is uncertain: one palaeontologist has suggested that they may have served to scoop snow into the mouth, since woolly mammoths would have needed to imbibe snow or ice in winter when no liquid water was available. The use of the tusks for breaking up ice for ingestion has also been proposed.

ABOVE Lyuba's milk tusk, shown at actual size. The root end is to the right, the protruding end to the left with its tiny cap of enamel. The milk tusk would have been shed after a few months.

Lyuba's tusks were present and one was extracted for study. These are, however, not the tusks that grew to such imposing size in adult mammoths, but the milk tusks that preceded them. A mere 4 cm (just over 1½ in) long, they had started to form before birth and would have been shed after a few months, had Lyuba survived, to be replaced by the permanent tusks that grew for the rest of an animal's life. The mammoth's tusks, like those of living elephants, are enlarged incisor teeth and grow out of the upper jaw. Formed of solid dentine (ivory), the permanent tusks typically reached 2.5 m (8 ft) in length, sometimes as

LEFT The skull of a mammoth from Ilford, Essex, England, showing the impressive, 2.5 m (8 ft) long tusks of an adult male. The tusks are held firmly within elongated sockets formed as outgrowths of the skull bone.

The first and second molar teeth extracted from Lyuba's jaw, shown at actual size. The first tooth (on the left) was slightly in wear; the second (on the right) had not yet erupted.

Jaw bones of three mammoths showing further stages in tooth progression. Left, aged 6, with third molar in wear and fourth erupting behind; centre, aged 25, with fifth molar in wear and sixth just visible behind; right, aged 45, with sixth (last) molar in full wear.

much as 4 m (13 ft) – longer than the animal was tall. About a third of that length was, however, buried in the jaw bone, anchoring the tusks in the skull. Mammoth tusks differ from those of living elephants in having a pronounced spiral shape. They emerged from the skull in a downward direction, then turned outward and upward in a wide arc, finally turning inward and occasionally crossing in front of the animal's head. In mammoths, both males and females possessed tusks, though those of males were substantially more massive. While they may have been used to break ice, clear snow, or to defend against predators, their principal function was in combat with other mammoths. The curved shapes would have interlocked, allowing the animals to engage in a powerful fight of pushing and twisting with their massive body weights behind them. This was graphically illustrated by a pair of bull mammoths found in Nebraska, which had evidently perished with their tusks irretrievably interlocked.

Teeth and tooth rings

Scans revealed the preservation of Lyuba's molar teeth in both upper and lower jaws, and these were removed from the left side during autopsy to allow further study. Mammoths had a series of six molar teeth in each jaw, but unlike most mammals these were not all present at the same time. Instead, like those of elephants, they replaced each other sequentially from behind, as described in Chapter 2. Indeed, the regular nature of this replacement has been used to 'age' the jaws of elephants, whether in life or in a museum collection. Lyuba's perfectly preserved teeth beautifully illustrate the start of this process in a mammoth's life. Her jaw contains the first three of the six molars, in different stages of formation. The first tooth, no bigger than a human molar, had erupted and had just started to wear; the second tooth, some 5 cm (2 in) long, lay behind it, still buried in the jaw; and behind that, the beginnings of the third tooth, still forming, and not due to erupt until the animal had reached 2 or 3 years of age.

In Lyuba's case, the diminutive first milk molar has proved a mine of information. The tooth was carefully sliced using a diamond saw, and under the microscope revealed growth lines, like tree rings, that mark out the days and weeks of the animal's life. One prominent line marked the time of the animal's birth. Following it, the daily increments of dentine, each around a hundredth of a millimetre wide, numbered around 35, indicating that Lyuba was only a month old when she died. Behind the birth line, however, growth lines indicate that the tooth had started to form as much as 16 months before birth, consistent with a total gestation of around 22 months as in living elephants. In a further study, isotopes of oxygen, nitrogen and carbon were analysed from each growth ring. Derived ultimately from the animal's food and drink, these vary seasonally with patterns of plant growth and rainfall, and suggest that Lyuba was born in the spring. It is possible, but not proven, that mammoths synchronized their breeding so that conception occurred mainly in the summer, with the result that the young would be born nearly 2 years later just as the plant growing season was getting underway and food became plentiful.

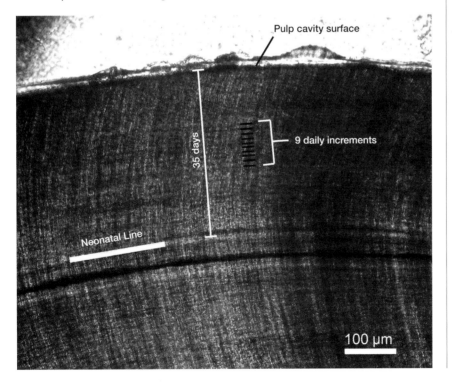

LEFT A magnified section through Lyuba's first molar; the white bar measures a tenth of a millimetre. The 'neonatal line' marks the time of Lyuba's birth; the increments above it, daily growth of dentine. Lyuba was around 35 days old when she died.

RIGHT Congealed, whitish-brown particles found in Lyuba's stomach and intestine. Chemical analysis shows these to be the remains of a milk meal suckled from her mother in the day or two before she died.

2 mm

In adult tusks, more widely spaced lines mark out the years. It is not possible to see a mammoth's entire life in a single tusk, because they wore away at the tip as they grew from the base, but the greatest number of annual rings yet seen is 42, consistent with a longevity of around 60 years seen in living elephants.

Lyuba's last meal

Lyuba's stomach was cylindrical and small, but contained numerous pieces of congealed whitish-brown material. Using a technique of chemical analysis known as infrared spectroscopy, the substance was shown to be saponified triglycerides – almost certainly the remains of partly digested milk. Similar particles were found in the intestine.

The plant food of adult mammoths – like that of elephants – was fermented and digested mostly in their enormous intestines. Lyuba's large intestine contained some plant material, mostly the stems and leaves of grasses or sedges, sheared into small fragments by parallel cuts at oblique angles. This is typical of grass chewed by adult elephants, but could not have been produced by Lyuba's just-erupted teeth, which had not yet worn to reveal the enamel bands capable of slicing up leaves in this way. Moreover, much of the plant matter in Lyuba's gut occurred in dense concentrations within a fine, brown organic matrix. It has been suggested, therefore, that Lyuba had been ingesting her mother's faeces. Such behaviour is known in living elephants, where baby animals ingest faeces to populate

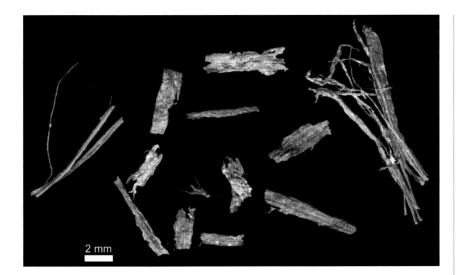

2 mm

LEFT Fragments of plant matter found in Lyuba's gut. These had evidently been cut up by chewing, but not necessarily by Lyuba herself. They may be the result of eating some of her mother's dung.

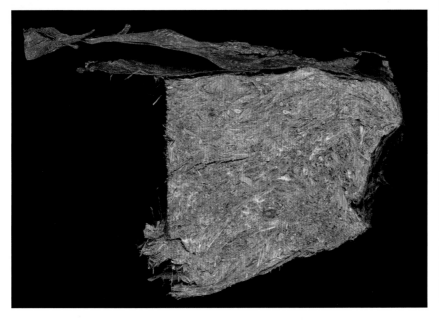

LEFT A slice of intestine from the Shandrin mammoth, an adult carcass excavated in 1972. The intestine wall, shrivelled and dark, surrounds a dense mass of plant food, providing direct information on the mammoth's diet.

their intestine with the microbes they need to ferment their food. Microscopic examination of Lyuba's gut contents also revealed spores of fungi specific to herbivore dung. Such spores had previously been identified in the gut of another individual, the Yukagir mammoth, but this animal was an adult. Here it suggested that the mammoth may have eaten dung to extract the maximum nutrients from its food – as rabbits do – perhaps during late winter when food was scarce.

More detailed examination of the plant material within Lyuba's gut – including the remains of seeds and fruits – gives a good picture of woolly mammoth food – whether it had been originally ingested by herself or by her mother. Species identified include grass, sedge, buttercups, wormwood, dwarf birch and mosses – a typical profile for the diverse grassland habitat known as 'steppe-tundra'. The

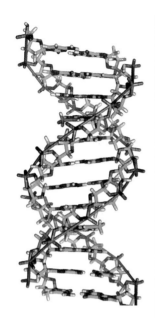

ABOVE A short section of a DNA molecule. The 'rungs' of the twisted 'ladder' comprise the base pairs, the letters of the DNA code that determine the growth and form of the organism.

sample also included remains of nematode worms, insects, mites, and even an arm bone of a vole! This material may have been inadvertently picked up while feeding either by Lyuba or (if the dung theory is correct) by her mother.

Several other frozen mammoths have preserved gut contents that have been studied. These, too, indicate a diet generally dominated by grasses and sedges. Variation among them may reflect seasonal changes in diet, or just what the individual animal happened to be feeding on in the day or so before it died. One carcass, the Shandrin mammoth, contained nearly 300 kg (650 lb) of food in its gut, showing that it had gorged on moss in its last days. The Yukagir mammoth, thought to have died in early spring, had browsed a significant quantity of willow.

DNA FROM MAMMOTHS

Even with the preservation of frozen carcasses, there are aspects of the mammoth's biology that are difficult or impossible to determine from simple observation. A revolution in our understanding of prehistoric creatures is, however, underway, based on the extraction of the minute quantities of DNA present in animal and plant remains from the Ice Age. DNA is the long-chain molecule present in all our cells that forms our genes and contains information for the growth and functioning of the organism. It differs between species according to their various adaptations, and also between individual organisms, determining the features by which they vary. These differences are largely encoded in the order of the molecular 'letters' (base-pairs) that are strung together to form the DNA chain. By decoding this sequence we can, in principle, learn about aspects of the organism not visible in its preserved remains.

DNA is a fragile molecule, and rapidly decays after the death of an organism. Early reports of DNA from dinosaur bones, tens of millions of years old, proved unfounded, and at present, we do not have any confirmed DNA from fossils older than a million years, with the vast majority less than 50,000 years old. This restricts serious study to remains from the Ice Age, but still encompasses many extinct species. The enemies of DNA preservation are warmth, moisture and oxygen, so remains locked in the arctic permafrost have proved to be particularly valuable sources of ancient DNA. The other major consideration when studying ancient DNA is the avoidance of contamination by related modern DNA, leading to misleading results. Ancient DNA research is therefore conducted in an ultra-clean laboratory separate from any laboratory where modern DNA is being analysed, with many precautions taken to exclude contamination and to test whether it has occurred.

Apart from humans, woolly mammoths have been the subject of the most intensive ancient DNA research. Early studies were aimed at determining the position of the mammoth in the evolutionary tree, and confirmed the mammoth's close relationship to the Asian elephant (see Chapter 1). Further studies have identified several populations within woolly mammoths, and have tracked their

fate in the countdown to extinction (see Chapter 5). A third, exciting line of enquiry is the reconstruction of the animal's appearance and adaptations, and this will be discussed below.

Hair colour

The first study attempting to reconstruct the mammoth's appearance from its DNA was targeted at its coat colour. Researchers selected a gene known to code for a protein that is key to the determination of hair colour in humans and other animals. The relevant portion of the gene is 1,236 base-pairs long, but, because DNA in the mammoth sample was fragmented into pieces of 140 base-pairs or less, the researchers extracted it as 23 segments and joined the sequences together. Every cell (apart from the sex cells) of a mammal contains two copies of each gene, and the researchers found that in the sampled mammoth one of the two copies differed from a modern elephant in its DNA sequence, in such a way that would have altered the structure of the resulting protein. They then constructed the variant protein in the laboratory and tested its properties. The changes had made it relatively inactive – precisely the effect known to result in pale hair in mice, horses and dogs. In a second study, however, a further 47 mammoths were analysed, and only one possessed a copy of the mutant gene. All the other individuals had the gene producing darker hair colour – probably dark brown. This, however, does not mean that most mammoths were uniformly dark in colour. Hair pigment

ABOVE An ancient DNA laboratory. Ultra-clean conditions are maintained, to avoid contamination of the ancient samples with modern DNA. The 'space suits' protect the samples from the scientists (particularly their DNA), rather than the other way round.

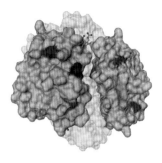

ABOVE Diagram of a haemoglobin molecule. On the left, the structure in a living elephant. On the right, the structure determined for the woolly mammoth. Differences are highlighted – these affect the performance of the molecule under different temperatures.

BELOW Prehistoric representation of two horses, in the cave of Pech Merle, southern France. Recent DNA work on ancient horse bones suggests the spots may be genuine rather than 'artistic licence'.

may have been deposited intermittently or in only certain areas. Recent research suggests the observed variation in mammoth hairs is genuine – some light, some dark, some even banded. Individual mammoths may have had a variegated or mottled appearance. Only the orange colour is probably artificial.

Haemoglobin

Another remarkable recent study has examined the mammoth's haemoglobin – the molecule in every mammal's red blood cells that collects oxygen from the lungs, transports it around the bloodstream, and transfers it to active tissues like muscles where it is needed. A haemoglobin molecule comprises four interlocking protein chains – two each of two kinds. Researchers extracted the DNA coding for both kinds of chain and then, using the mammoth's gene sequence, manufactured its haemoglobin proteins in the laboratory. One of the mammoth's protein chains was found to have three differences (mutations) compared to living elephants, which significantly altered the shape of the molecule. What effect this may have had on its function was then explored by running standard tests, as though it were a blood sample in a medical laboratory. In particular, the researchers investigated the effect of temperature on the ability of the haemoglobin to release its cargo of oxygen. Modern elephant haemoglobin can release its oxygen under warm conditions, for example at the site of exercising muscles. Under cold conditions, however, the oxygen remains bound to the haemoglobin molecule. The experiment showed that mammoth

haemoglobin was able to release its oxygen under lower temperatures than in the living elephants – a likely adaptation to an arctic climate, where the limbs and other extremities would have been cold and yet needed oxygen to function. The study of ancient DNA has thus added a physiological adaptation to the observable adaptations of mammoths to the cold – its fur and its fat layers.

Other species

Researchers are also starting to fill out details of other Ice Age species. A recent study of wild horses from the last glacial period has shown that they had a variety of coat colours. Sampling over 30 horse fossils from Europe, Siberia and North America, some of them dating back as far as 35,000 years ago, researchers examined nine different genes associated with coat colour. They found that some individuals had a bay coat, others black, while a third group shared a gene associated with 'leopard spotting', dark spots on a pale background. The latter finding is particularly significant because some horse representations in cave art show spotted coats, but some archaeologists had suggested that this was symbolic or abstract. Other horses in Palaeolithic art are painted pale or black, so it seems that the prehistoric artists were simply drawing the variety they had seen in nature.

Could mammoths walk again?

The discovery that DNA is preserved in the remains of mammoths and other Ice Age species has raised the question of bringing long-extinct creatures back to life. Several possible methods have been suggested, although in reality scientists are very far from being able to enact any of them, even if it were desirable to do so.

In all proposed methods, the living Asian elephant plays a key role, chosen because it is the closest living relative of the mammoth. In the first idea, a sperm

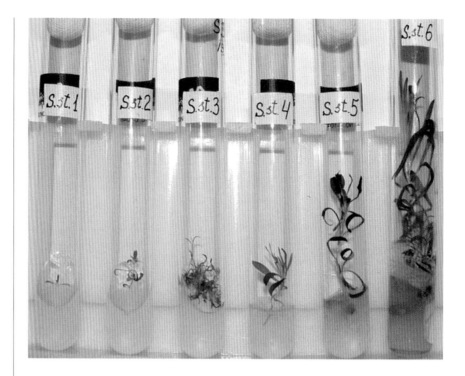

cell from a male mammoth carcass would be used to fertilize an egg cell recovered from a female elephant. The procedure would take place in a laboratory dish as in human in-vitro fertilization (IVF). The embryo would then be returned to the elephant's womb, where it would implant and grow. A chief problem with this idea is that the resulting creature would be a hybrid, genetically half-elephant and half-mammoth. Whether it would even develop properly or survive is open to question, as occasional crosses between African and Asian elephants in zoos were malformed and died soon after birth. If the 50% mammoth survived, however, the idea would be to cross it with another mammoth cell, producing a 75% mammoth, and so on for multiple generations until – eventually – a virtually pure mammoth resulted.

The next suggested method is cloning, inspired by the successful cloning of sheep and other domestic animals. Here the egg cell of a female elephant would again be taken, but this time its nucleus – the part of the cell containing the majority of its DNA – would be removed. In its place would be inserted the nucleus of a mammoth, taken from one of its body cells. The resulting cell would be stimulated, either electrically or chemically, to start division, and would be replaced into the mother elephant to continue its growth. The resulting animal would be a clone of – genetically identical to –the original mammoth. This is a distinct advantage over the IVF method, but even with the cloning of living species such as mice and sheep, there are multiple failures before a healthy individual is produced. Moreover, the egg cell around the nucleus also influences the makeup of the resulting animal, and the effect of putting a mammoth nucleus into an elephant's egg is unknown.

Both of these methods further suffer from a major practical problem: in all mammoth remains tested so far, the DNA is broken up into millions of tiny fragments, a result of decay over its long burial. In order for a cell to produce a new individual, whether by IVF or cloning, the nucleus would have to be virtually intact, with the DNA preserved in its original chains of millions of base-pairs, and organized into chromosomes – the structures inside the nucleus which house the DNA. Thus far we have not found any mammoth cells that are remotely as well preserved as this. A recent breakthrough by Russian scientists has given some pause for thought: they grew living examples of a small flowering plant from fruit tissue 30,000 years old recovered from the Siberian permafrost deposits, similar to those which contain mammoth remains. The plant cells may have preserved viable DNA because they are enclosed in rigid cellulose walls that have protected their contents, unlike animal cells that lack cellulose walls and are more exposed to decay. Nonetheless, these findings make it slightly less implausible that a viable mammoth cell might one day be found.

Recent developments in genetics have suggested a third way in which a living mammoth might be produced, one which circumvents the shattered nature of DNA in most frozen tissue. By extracting all of the DNA fragments from a sample of mammoth tissue, the entire DNA sequence of the mammoth – some 3 billion bases – could be determined, but in small, random sections typically 100 bases long. Using the elephant gene sequence as a guide, the mammoth sequences could be 'stitched together' in a computer to give the complete original sequence. It is estimated that this would differ from the elephant's own sequence at about 400,000 of the base positions. Then a living elephant cell would be taken, and one by one those bases would be artificially altered to the condition seen in the mammoth. Effectively, the gene sequence of a mammoth would have been engineered. The egg would be implanted back in the mother elephant, and 22 months later a woolly mammoth would be born. Fortunately or unfortunately, depending on one's view, such methods are well beyond current technical possibility.

Even if all the technical hurdles could be overcome, ethical objections have been raised to such schemes. The mammoth was – like the living elephants – a highly intelligent animal, adapted to a complex group life, and whose natural habitat has disappeared. To resurrect the species just to keep a few individuals in captivity for public sensation or scientific glory could be considered a dubious undertaking. Secondly, the world is facing the likely extinction of thousands of species by human action. The living elephants are themselves under threat, with a report of May 2013 estimating that up to 35,000 elephants a year are being illegally killed in Africa (see Chapter 5). Stemming the tide of ongoing destruction should be our priority, rather than expending considerable effort and resources attempting to resurrect already extinct species.

ABOVE Fully-grown plant of *Silene stenophylla* cloned from preserved tissue. The plant is identical to living examples except for somewhat longer and more widely-spaced petals.

CHAPTER 5
Endangered and extinct

THE EXTINCTION OF THE MAMMOTHS AND MASTODONS has been the subject of intense debate since the species were first discovered more than 200 years ago, and even today this issue is not fully resolved, with researchers continuing to argue over contending explanations. The disappearance of these animals cannot be viewed in isolation as it was part of a major phase of extinction of large mammals ('megafauna') that started around the middle of the last glaciation. Roughly in the period 50,000–4,000 years ago, numerous large-mammal species died out in many parts of the world. In Europe and Asia, the woolly rhinoceros, giant deer, cave bear and cave lion were among the casualties, in addition to the woolly mammoth. North America lost some 40 species of large mammal, or 70% of its total, including the giant sloths, glyptodonts, and various species of deer, horse and camel, as well as the Columbian mammoth and mastodon. South America and Australia suffered proportionally even higher losses. The only parts of the world left relatively untouched were Africa and southern Asia, the regions where today it is still possible to see 'megafauna', including elephants and rhinoceroses, in the wild.

Despite its impact, the extinction of the late Ice Age does not rank alongside the mass extinctions of earlier epochs, such as the event some 65 million years ago which saw the extinction of the dinosaurs. Those mass extinctions affected a much higher proportion of Earth's total biota, including both animals and plants, species of all sizes from the gigantic to the microscopic, and inhabitants of the oceans, rivers and lakes as well as those living on land. The extinction of the late Ice Age, by contrast, was highly selective, affecting only large mammals – those over around 40 kg (90 lb) in body weight, about the size of a fallow deer or pronghorn antelope. Nonetheless, the event had widespread repercussions, both in terms of the landscapes on which the megafauna had formerly roamed, and on the humans that had lived alongside them.

As with the extinction of the dinosaurs, various theories have been proposed to account for Ice Age megafaunal extinctions. The main contenders are, on the one hand, natural climate change and its effects on habitats and, on the other, hunting by people. Other suggested causes include disease and meteorite impact.

OPPOSITE **The co-existence of mammoths and people is graphically illustrated in prehistoric art. In this striking image, from Chauvet Cave, France, the tusks were drawn first and then engraved. The image shows a mammoth with its tail raised, apparently about to defaecate.**

ABOVE Woolly mammoths on their rich grassland habitat. According to one theory of extinction, climate change at the end of the last glaciation led to the disappearance of this environment and the mammal species that depended on it.

Any satisfactory explanation must account not only for the extinctions but also for why some species died out while others survived.

The extinction of so many spectacular animals in the very recent geological past has particular resonance today. Due largely to human impacts, many species today are threatened with extinction. These include the closest living relatives of the mammoth and mastodon, the elephants. A combination of habitat destruction and poaching has severely reduced the numbers of both the African and Asian elephant. Can any parallels be drawn between the threats facing the living elephants, and those which drove their prehistoric relatives to extinction? Can we learn something from the events of the past to help us conserve the species that are still with us?

Here we focus on three of the elephant relatives to become extinct in the Ice Age: the woolly mammoth, Columbian mammoth and American mastodon. Before considering the evidence for the different causes of their demise, we have to establish exactly where and when each species died out.

TRACKING THE DIE-OUT

It was originally believed that the extinction of the megafauna was a single event in which all species disappeared at more or less the same time – around the transition from the last glaciation to the present interglacial, now dated to 11,700 years ago. While many species did go extinct at roughly this time, research has increasingly shown that the global pattern was staggered, some species (such as giant wombats and kangaroos in Australia) dying out as long ago as 40,000 years ago, with others, such as the Irish Elk in northern Eurasia, surviving as recently as 8,000 years ago – well into the present interglacial.

Based on fossil occurrences, the total range of mammoths, woolly and Columbian combined, has been estimated at around 20 million km² (nearly 8 million square miles). For the American mastodon, restricted mainly to wooded areas of the USA and Mexico, the figure is around 3 million km² (just over 1 million square miles). It is very difficult to estimate numbers of animals living at any time in the past, as the density of fossils is strongly influenced by other factors such as the likelihood of being preserved, but based on the historical density of living elephants in Africa and Asia, there may have been as many as 6 million mammoths and a million mastodons alive in their heyday.

Our principal tool for tracing the demise of these once-flourishing populations is radiocarbon dating. This method can in principle date, to within a few tens or hundreds of years, any organic remains from about 50,000 years ago until almost the present. A few grams of bone, tooth or tusk are sampled, and in the laboratory are cleaned, ground up, and collagen extracted. Collagen is one of the main proteins found within bone. It is the same molecule that forms tendons and sinews and is relatively resilient, but with time it may have degraded depending on the conditions of burial, in which case the specimen cannot be dated by this means. Where present, however, it is the carbon atoms within the collagen that are the target of measurement. Radiocarbon dating relies upon the steady transformation of a rare form (isotope) of carbon, carbon-14, into nitrogen. We know the rate of decay of carbon-14, so the proportion of carbon-14 left in the sample, compared to the commoner carbon-12, can be used to calculate the time that elapsed since the organism died.

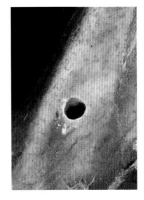

BELOW A well-preserved woolly mammoth molar from St Lawrence Island, off Alaska. A hole drilled at the top of a root (arrowed and seen in close up above) produced dentine powder from which collagen and DNA was successfully extracted.

To trace the extinction of a species like the woolly mammoth, hundreds of fossils from across its geographical range have been radiocarbon-dated. These give a wide range of ages – from beyond the limit of the method (more than about 50,000 years old) to only a few thousand years old. The principle of the study is that the most recent date obtained provides our best estimate of when the species went extinct – it is the point after which there is no further

evidence of the species' existence. Such conclusions suffer from the problem of 'negative evidence' – it is always possible that the next sample will prove to be more recent than the latest previously known – but by dating more and more samples, we arrive ever closer to the true date of extinction.

A further important feature of this method is that it allows us to examine whether a species went extinct across its whole range at once, or contracted step by step over a period of time, finally dying out from a last refuge. This is possible by looking at the pattern of radiocarbon dates for different regions of the species' range: is the latest date the same everywhere, or did the species die out in different places at different times?

A second, and very recent, line of evidence is provided by the study of preserved DNA. As well as enlightening us about the relationships and adaptations of Ice Age species (see Chapter 4), DNA data can also provide clues to the process of their extinction. In particular, changes in the number of animals living at a given time, very difficult to establish from mere fossil abundance, can be estimated by looking at DNA sequences from a series of individuals. In general, the greater the degree of DNA variation, the more numerous the original population. It is also possible to extrapolate DNA evidence backward, using the genetic diversity within a population to estimate when that population arose. Finally, the degree of genetic difference between populations can provide an estimate of when those populations split from each other.

THE IMPACT OF CLIMATE

According to the climatic theory of extinction, it was changes in global climate that led to the loss of the megafauna, including the mammoths and mastodons. It is beyond doubt that natural climate change, driven by the processes described in Chapter 3, has had profound effects on the Earth and its biota over the past 50,000 years. The greatest expansion of the polar ice-sheets took place between 25,000 and 20,000 years ago. Even after they had retreated somewhat, the climate remained cool, until around 14,700 years ago, when average temperature warmed very rapidly, by around 6°C (about 11°F), to levels close to those of today. Temperatures

RIGHT Climate curve for the past 80,000 years. A strong warming spike at 14,700 years ago (left arrow) was followed by a return to cold until the final warming into the present interglacial at 11,700 years ago (right arrow).

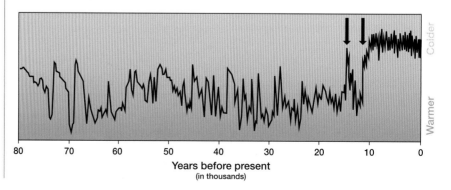

Years before present
(in thousands)

LEFT The northern part of the woolly mammoth's former range is today tundra – short, slow-growing vegetation supporting reindeer and some other species, but unsuitable for large grazers like the mammoth.

LEFT The southern part of the woolly mammoth's former range is today coniferous forest, suitable for moose (shown here) and other browsing species, but not for large grazers like the mammoth.

then declined again, over a period of nearly 2,000 years, until they were back at glacial levels and the ice-sheets re-expanded for a while. Finally, at around 11,700 years ago, there was a second rapid warming that brought the world into the present interglacial. Climate has remained relatively stable since then, with minor changes such as a cool 'blip' around 8,200 years ago, and the 'Little Ice Age' of the sixteenth to seventeenth centuries.

Although climate can directly influence large mammals, it is the indirect effects of climate on vegetation that most affect the mammals' range and abundance, especially for the herbivores. As described in Chapter 3, it was the rich

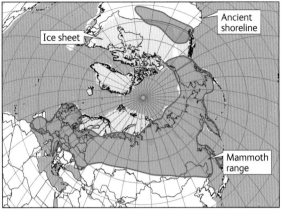

A – 40,000 years ago

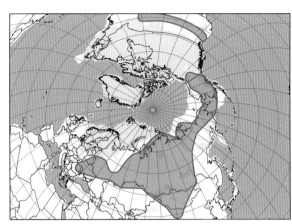

B – 20,000 years ago

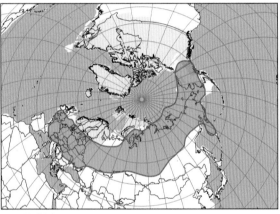

C – 15,000 years ago

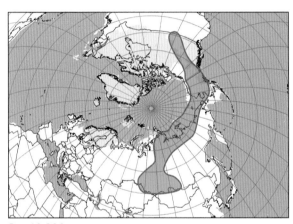

D – 13,000 years ago

ABOVE Maps showing the shifting distribution of the woolly mammoth in the countdown to its extinction. Ice sheets are shown in grey, and changes in sea level are indicated by the shifting shoreline.

and varied open grasslands of northern latitudes that provided sustenance to the woolly mammoth and other grazing species during the last glaciation. When the climate warmed, starting at around 14,700 years ago, this vast ecosystem began to collapse, the grasslands being replaced, eventually, by today's zonation of tundra in the north and forest in the south. The climatic theory of extinction proposes that the woolly mammoth's range and numbers contracted as its grassland habitat disappeared, until the species was squeezed out entirely.

Countdown to extinction

To test these ideas, we can compare the timing of habitat changes with the pattern of contraction in range and numbers of woolly mammoths. Firstly, DNA data suggests that mammoth populations were squeezed down to small numbers in the last major warm period (interglacial) around 120,000 years ago, but this did not lead to extinction, and the populations rapidly expanded again as the last glaciation

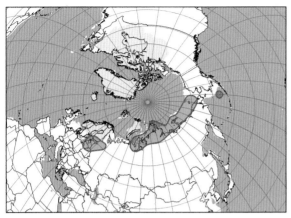

E – 12,000 years ago

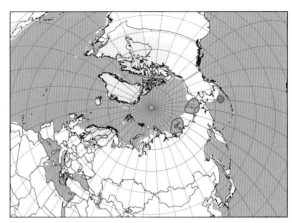

F – 11,000 years ago

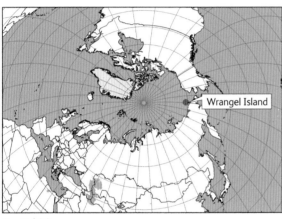

Wrangel Island

G – 5,000 years ago

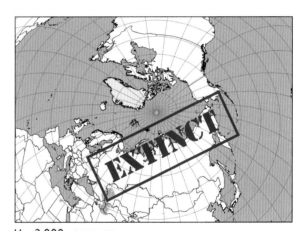

H – 3,000 years ago

began. From around 40,000 years ago we can plot the changing distribution of the mammoth using the radiocarbon data.

The maps show that from then until around 20,000 years ago, the range of the mammoth continued mostly unbroken from Britain in the west, across Europe and northern Asia (Siberia), and via the Bering land connection to Alaska (USA) and the Yukon (Canada) (map A). This was the 'heyday' of the woolly mammoth. There are hints of range shifts during this period – for example, a temporary retreat to the north in Siberia between 35,000 and 30,000 years ago. This may have been the cause of a decline in genetic diversity that, according to DNA evidence, started as early as 30,000 years ago, and may have reduced the adaptability of the mammoth and its ability to survive the challenges that were to come.

A major contraction of the mammoth's range started around 21,500 years ago, when mammoths evacuated most of Europe for around 2,000 years (map B). This coincides exactly with the maximum expansion of the European ice-sheets, which would have had a marked effect on the vegetation productivity in the region, and could explain the mammoth's contraction to the east at this time. Once the ice had retreated somewhat, the mammoths reclaimed most of their former range (map C), but DNA evidence suggests that this apparently healthy situation may have been deceptive. The genetic data point to a huge decline in mammoth numbers, by a factor of 10 or more, beginning about 20,000–15,000 years ago. This indicates a major thinning of the mammoth population, even while its geographic range remained extensive.

The major warming at 14,700 years ago did not immediately affect the mammoth's range, but just under a thousand years later the species died out across half its Eurasian range, remaining only in eastern Siberia. The explanation for the delay is that the forests, which had contracted to the south during the glaciation, took time to spread northward. The 'starting gun' was fired when the climate warmed at 14,700 years ago, but only at around 13,900 years ago did the forests reach northern Europe, coinciding closely with the disappearance of the mammoths as their grassland habitat was squeezed out (map D). As forests spread across Siberia, so the mammoth's range contracted there too, until by 12,800 years ago it occupied only the northernmost, arctic rim of Siberia (map E). Around the same time the woolly mammoth also became extinct in North America, at least according to the radiocarbon data. However, a controversial DNA study has suggested survival in central Alaska for a further 2,000 years. The study was based on woolly mammoth DNA extracted from soil samples dated to only 10,500 years old, and requires confirmation from directly dated mammoth bones.

Around 12,800 years ago the climate became colder again, a 'last gasp' of glacial conditions that lasted around a thousand years. The forests retreated somewhat, and we see a corresponding minor re-expansion of the mammoth's range into the northeast fringes of Europe. By 11,000 years ago, however, the climate had finally warmed into the present interglacial and the mammoth was left only in extreme northern outposts (map F) that subsequently became islands as the sea level rose. One by one these isolated populations died out: first on the New Siberian Islands north of the Siberian mainland (last record 10,700 years ago), then St Paul Island off the coast of Alaska (last record 6,500 years ago), and finally on Wrangel Island off the extreme northeast of Siberia (map G, last record 4,000 years ago). An intriguing piece of DNA evidence has come from a study of the Wrangel Island population. The mammoths there do not, surprisingly, show any reduction in numbers in the run-up to their extinction 4,000 years ago. The data suggest that the population was stable at around a few thousand individuals until the very end – so the final collapse, whatever caused it – was sudden rather than gradual.

Summing up, the DNA and radiocarbon evidence shows clearly that the extinction of the woolly mammoth was not an instantaneous event but was a complex story of successive expansions and contractions over a long period, the range ultimately contracting and fragmenting into smaller and smaller areas until the last population died out (map H). It also shows that many of the range shifts correspond closely to known variations in climate and vegetation.

Extinction of the Columbian mammoth and mastodon

For the Columbian mammoth and mastodon, further south in North America, the situation is more difficult to read. The climatic changes of the late Ice Age certainly had major impacts on the landscape there too. Formerly lush areas of the west and southwest, in present-day Arizona for example, became semi-desert and unable to support anything like the diversity and biomass of mammals that had lived there previously. Other regions turned from a mixed, diverse parkland vegetation with a rich mammal fauna to an expanse of monotonous grassland of a type suited only to specialist grazers like bison.

The disappearance of the Columbian mammoth and mastodon falls broadly within the cycle of climate changes at the end of the last glaciation, but we have far fewer radiocarbon dates to go on, and insufficient DNA data thus far, to be sure whether the changes correspond to specific climatic effects as they do for the woolly mammoth. Existing dates suggest a more rapid and synchronous collapse across much of these species' ranges than for their woolly cousin. In areas as widespread as Alberta, Wyoming and Oklahoma, and even for the dwarf mammoths of Santa Rosa, California (see Chapter 1), the latest dates for Columbian mammoth fall in the narrow interval 13,000–12,700 years ago. Terminal dates for the mastodon, in its strongholds in the east and midwest of the USA, are almost identical to these. However, some researchers have suggested that numbers in both species had begun to decline earlier than that. They used an unusual measure of animal abundance – a fungus that grows only on the dung of large herbivores, the presence of which can be identified in ancient deposits by its preserved spores. At sites in New York and Indiana it was found that there was a major reduction in the quantity of fungal spores between

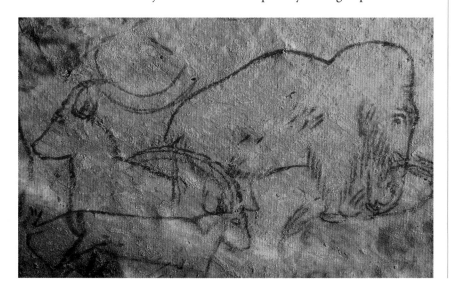

LEFT Drawing of a mammoth, a metre across, on the ceiling of Rouffignac Cave, France. Although the line of the head and back seems crude, there is great attention to detail in the eye, hair, foot and trunk tip.

around 14,800 and 13,700 years ago, a thousand years or more before the latest radiocarbon dates for mammoth and mastodon. This is a rather crude tool as it cannot distinguish between different mammal species, but the researchers concluded that something had caused the populations of all megafaunal species to collapse, at least in that area, by around 14,000 years ago. This could be connected with the global warming that started at 14,700 years ago, but the precise link is unclear. On the other hand, the final radiocarbon dates for the Columbian mammoth and mastodon fall around the start of the cold snap 12,800 thousand years ago. These climate changes are likely to have reduced mammoth and mastodon habitats to smaller areas. Even so, with diets less tied to a vanished habitat than the woolly mammoth's, it is more difficult to see why these species might not have survived somewhere among the diverse habitats remaining within the North American continent.

MAMMOTHS, MASTODONS AND HUMANS

Did humans play a role in the global disappearance of the megafauna, including the two species of mammoth and the mastodon? Humans certainly had a long history of coexistence with mammoths and their relatives. The origin and early evolution of the human and elephant families show remarkable parallels, each beginning in Africa around 7 million years ago and there diversifying into several species, some of which later spread to the rest of the world. With the advent of modern humans, *Homo sapiens*, and their spread into Europe around 40,000 years ago, we have a wealth of tangible evidence of the importance of the woolly mammoth in the lives of our ancestors.

Mammoth art

Caves in France, Spain and elsewhere contain priceless works of art from the Ice Age, with large mammals as their dominant theme. The art covers almost the whole period of modern-human occupation of Ice Age Europe, from around 35,000 to 11,500 years ago. Some 500 prehistoric representations of the woolly mammoth have been found on the walls of around 50 caves, although three caves in the south of France include almost half of the images. The commonest method of depicting the mammoths was engraving onto a bare rock face without the use of pigments. Other mammoths were drawn as a red or black outline, and finally in some cases part or all of their body was painted in. The representations range from sketchy, to deliberately stylized, to highly naturalistic. In the latter examples, many features of mammoth anatomy can be seen that correspond to evidence from finds of frozen carcasses. The domed head and sloping back are usually expressed, fur is commonly represented, and the strongly curved tusks are often prominent. More detailed features (including the double trunk-tip, see p.101) or behavioural moments (such as a raised tail that precisely replicates that of an elephant about to defaecate, see p.92) are occasionally visible.

As common as mammoths on cave walls are 'portable mammoths' – engravings on small pieces of bone, stone or ivory, or sculpted mammoths of the same materials. Many are known from cave sites in Europe, but in 2011 the first authenticated prehistoric representation of a mammoth from North America was announced. Found by an amateur fossil hunter near Vero Beach, Florida, the mammoth was carved onto a 38 cm (15-inch) piece of bone and is around 13,000 years old. From its location in the southern USA, it very likely represents a Columbian mammoth – another first.

Portable mammoths sometimes even had a function. At Montastruc, a rock shelter in the south of France inhabited by people around 13,000 years ago, a small sculpted mammoth was found among the archaeological remains. The

ABOVE AND BELOW A length of reindeer antler was used to carve this 13 cm (5 in) long mammoth, its head and trunk lowered, its tusks directed forward and cradling a 'handle'. Found at Montastruc rock shelter in France, it functioned as a spear-thrower (see above).

ABOVE From Montastruc, some 13,000 years old, the ivory 'swimming reindeer' is considered a masterpiece of Ice Age art. The female, with smaller body and antlers, is in front; the male follows behind. The natural curvature and taper indicate that the piece was carved from a carefully-selected portion of tusk near to the tip.

object, carved from reindeer antler, looks like a very stylised mammoth, but this is because it was, in fact, the carved end of a practical object: a so-called spear-thrower. Instead of grasping the wooden shaft of a spear, prehistoric people found that a longer throw could be achieved by fitting the end of the spear loosely onto the hook of a separate item, a spear-thrower, which was kept in the hand as the arm was drawn back and thrust forward, releasing the spear javelin-style (see previous page). In the Montastruc thrower, a small hook on the mammoth's back received the hollowed end of the spear, and a shaft emerging from the front of the carved mammoth and including its tusks, now broken, would have been grasped.

Mammoth DIY

Mammoth products were themselves put to practical use by prehistoric people, and, indeed, across much of central and eastern Europe mammoth seems to have been the major resource of people for thousands of years, especially in the interval 25,000–15,000 years ago. Mammoth bone was carved into beautifully formed spoons and spatulas found at Avdeevo in European Russia, and into a spear-point at a Neanderthal site in northern Germany. In a rare example from the New World, an extraordinary giant chopping tool was formed from part of a mammoth shoulder-blade. Found in South Dakota at a site where Columbian mammoths had been butchered, its sharpened edge had been formed by flaking away pieces of bone.

However, the most prized resource was ivory. Mammoth tusk was carved with great skill into a plethora of objects, including small sculptures of real or imaginary animals, statuettes of women (the so-called 'Venus' figurines), beads and other jewellery.

RIGHT A huge chopping tool crafted from a mammoth's scapula, this unique find was made at the Lange-Ferguson site in South Dakota, USA, where an adult and juvenile mammoth had evidently been butchered by Clovis hunters some 13,000 years ago.

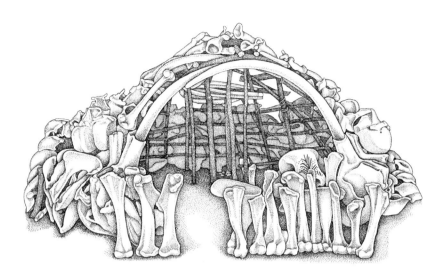

At Montastruc, a gently curving section of woolly mammoth tusk had been carved into two exquisite reindeer, head to tail, generally thought to have been represented as swimming. Practical objects include an ivory flute from a cave in southern Germany, and the world's oldest boomerang. Found in a cave in Poland and dated to around 21,000 years old, the boomerang is 70 cm (28 inches) long and carved with great skill into an aerofoil shape. Experiments with replicas show that it is a non-returning boomerang, a type that travels very fast in a straight line and could hit a prey animal at a range of 200 m (650 ft) or more.

Most spectacular of all are the mammoth-bone huts of eastern Europe. With few trees to provide wood, prehistoric people turned to mammoth bones for building materials. In southwest Russia, the Ukraine and Poland, archaeologists have excavated large circular structures made of hundreds of mammoth bones and interpreted as huts. They were usually arranged in groups – up to five have been found in one area – forming a small village. Remarkable numbers of mammoth bones were used to make each structure. In one hut at Mezhirich in the Ukraine, for example, 25 skulls formed the inner wall, pointing down with their tusk sockets embedded in the ground. Over 60 massive leg bones and 35 tusks formed the rest of the structure, surrounded by an outer wall formed from the mandibles (lower jaws) of no fewer than 95 mammoths. The hut was probably shaped like an igloo – now collapsed – and is believed to have been originally covered with animal hides.

Until recently, it was assumed that the mammoth-bone villages were made only by the modern people (*Homo sapiens*) who entered Europe around 40,000 years ago. However, recent excavations in the Ukraine have revealed that a remarkably similar technology was apparently devised by Neanderthals (*Homo neanderthalensis*): the site is dated to 44,000 years ago and is full of stone tools of Neanderthal type. The excavators uncovered a pit filled with bones, different areas for activities such as butchering and tool production, and a circular structure made of mammoth bones and interpreted as a dwelling.

ABOVE **A prehistoric encounter with a group of woolly mammoths. While mammoths were clearly hunted at times, the degree to which this contributed to their extinction is unclear.**

HUNTING – A CAUSE OF EXTINCTION?

Although it is clear that people commonly used mammoth products, the extent to which they actually hunted them is a contentious issue among archaeologists. In the southwest USA, for example, some sites where mammoth bones and stone tools were found together were originally interpreted as kill sites, but the remains may simply have been washed together by river action. In other cases, mammoth bones were more obviously accumulated by humans. At the Colby site in Wyoming, human artefacts were found together with hundreds of Columbian mammoth bones stacked in ways that are hard to interpret as due to natural forces. At the site of La Cotte on Jersey (today an island in the English Channel but during the last glaciation part of the mainland), hundreds of mammoth and woolly rhino bones were found inside a cave, partially sorted in piles of different bone types.

At some sites there is evidence of the butchering of mammoth carcasses, presumably for food. In the remains of skeletons found in Wisconsin, some bones bear marks indicating that flesh was cut away using stone tools. At the Kimmswick Bone Bed in Missouri – the same locality where Albert Koch had unearthed a mastodon skeleton in 1840 (see Chapter 2) – archaeologists in 1979 found mastodon bones and spear points together in the same level. They also discovered remnants of a campfire and thousands of small stone flakes — fragments resulting from the sharpening of stone tools. It is likely that hunters skinned and butchered a dead mastodon using tools manufactured and re-sharpened at the site.

These activities do not necessarily point to hunting, however. Like other predatory animals, prehistoric humans may have been scavenging already-dead carcasses, rather than killing the living animal. They might, for example, have used flaming torches to scare off predators like lions from their kills. For building purposes, even dry bones may have been collected. The mammoth-bone huts of eastern Europe might at first suggest that humans were killing mammoths in large numbers – the Mezhirich hut containing the remains of at least 95 individuals. But radiocarbon dating of the bones suggests that the animals had died at very different times – some of them hundreds or even thousands of years before their bones were used for building purposes. The stone-age people of 18,000 years ago were, in effect, early palaeontologists, excavating the remains of long-dead animals.

ABOVE Set a mammoth to catch a mammoth: part of a woolly mammoth scapula found at the Yana site in northern Siberia, with fragments of both stone and mammoth ivory embedded within the puncture, suggesting a complex projectile point.

Evidence for hunting

Yet humans did hunt mammoths and mastodons, at least occasionally. The most convincing evidence comes from two extraordinary finds made in recent years in Russia. The first, announced in 2013, was made at the Yana River site in northern Siberia where hundreds of mammoth remains have been excavated. Among them, one scapula (shoulder-blade) of a young mammoth had been pierced by a stone point, again indicating a thrust to the chest region, while a second contained fragments of both stone and ivory, suggesting an ivory spearhead edged with sharp stone flakes. The finds are around 32,000 years old. At the second site, Lugovskoye in southern Siberia, a mammoth vertebra was discovered that had been pierced by a stone spearhead which had broken off leaving the remains of the flint spear

LEFT The Yana archaeological site, where hundreds of mammoth bones, stone tools, and other artefacts indicate substantial human dependence on mammoths in the area 32,000 years ago.

embedded in the bone. The vertebra was from the chest region of the animal, indicating a thrust aimed at the heart or lungs. Calculations suggest that to penetrate bone so deeply, the hunter must have been no more than 5 m (16½ ft) from the animal. The find dates from around 16,500 years ago.

In 1977, remarkable evidence of a mastodon hunt was unearthed at the Manis site in Washington State. Here, the tip of a bone projectile point was found embedded in a rib of a mastodon skeleton. In a recent twist, DNA analysis has shown that the projectile point, which would have been hafted to a wooden shaft, had itself been manufactured from a mastodon bone – a mastodon used to catch a mastodon.

That such finds are rare does not itself mean that hunting the mammoth and mastodon were uncommon practices, since to find such direct evidence preserved at archaeological sites would be unusual in any event. Scientists have therefore devised more circumstantial means of addressing the question. Examining the 'medical chart' revealed by tusk rings (see Chapter 4) is one such approach. Mammoths, like living elephants, lived in small herds comprising related adult females and their young. On reaching maturity, adolescent males left the herd to lead a more solitary life, while females stayed within it. The age at which animals reached maturity shows up in the tusk record as a period of stress: for males, when they first left their mother's herd and had to fend for themselves; for females, when they first gave birth. Scientists reason that if extinction were caused by climate change, late populations would be under food stress, which would slow their growth and reproduction, so they would reach sexual maturity later. If they were being hunted, on the other hand, they might mature sooner as natural selection would favour individuals that bred younger, before they were killed. Males could also breed younger because there was less competition from older, dominant bulls. The small number of mastodon tusks examined so far provides tentative support for the hunting theory: in animals dated older than 13,000 years ago maturity is indicated at between 11 and 15 years old, whereas the individuals after 13,000 years ago – close to the time of extinction – had matured at 11–12 years. The results are intriguing but more data are needed to confirm the hypothesis.

We also need to consider the likely hunting behaviour of prehistoric people. Hunting an animal as large and dangerous as a mammoth or mastodon would have been a risky business, even if groups of hunters co-operated as they almost certainly did. There was plentiful smaller game in the Ice Age world, such as bison, horse and reindeer (caribou), and, while still potentially dangerous to hunt, they were presumably less so than a 6-tonne mammoth or mastodon armed with formidable tusks. Some archaeologists have argued that the benefits of a successful mammoth or mastodon hunt, both in terms of the huge resources offered by a single carcass as well as the social status accrued, still made hunting these animals an attractive proposition. Even so, occasional hunting of a species does not necessarily lead to its extinction, let alone that of numerous other species that became extinct around the same time.

To explore this question, some scientists have set up a mammoth-hunting 'game' on a computer. Starting with, say, 3 million virtual mammoths across the North American continent, relatively small bands of virtual humans are allowed to hunt mammoths at a predefined rate (such as one animal per person per month). Taking into account the likely rate of the animals' reproduction, and growth of the human population, these models suggested that hunting **could** have caused the extinction of various species within several hundred to a thousand years. Other researchers, however, have criticized the models for being unrealistic about animal (and human) behaviour. In present-day Africa, for example, elephants in areas under heavy poaching soon learn extreme vigilance against human hunters, keeping away from people and avoiding areas where other elephants have been killed. It is likely mammoths and mastodons would have behaved similarly. Hunters, also, even if they had been proboscidean specialists, would have switched to other prey once the mammoths and mastodons became scarce, so it seems unlikely they would have brought any one species fully to extinction.

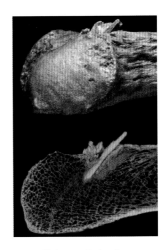

ABOVE Set a mastodon to catch a mastodon: the rib of a mastodon excavated at Manis, Washington State, USA, with a projectile point made of mastodon bone embedded within it. Above: outside view; below: X-ray.

CLIMATE CHANGE PLUS HUNTING EQUALS EXTINCTION?

It seems clear that the ranges of many megafaunal species were affected, and often severely reduced, by the natural changes in climate and vegetation toward the end of the last glaciation. However, as explained in Chapter 3, there had been many similar cycles of climate change throughout the Ice Age. These did result in the loss of a few mammal species with each major glaciation, but the scale of the extinction around the time of the last one far exceeded anything seen before. This suggests that a purely climatic explanation for the losses may be incomplete.

ABOVE A replica spear of the type used by 'Clovis' hunters in North America 12–13,000 years ago. The stone point has been bound to the wooden shaft using animal sinews; this would have been attached to a longer wooden shaft for use.

The spread of modern humans

There is a broad coincidence of timing between the arrival of modern people in different parts of the world, and the loss of the megafauna. Australia came first, some time around 50,000–40,000 years ago; then the Americas, between about 14,000 and 12,000 years ago (see below); and in the last 2,000 years many species of mammals and birds were lost from the islands of Madagascar, New Zealand and the West Indies as they became colonized by humans. The pattern breaks down for Eurasia, however: there, people had been present for over a million years, but megafaunal extinctions accelerated only in the last 100,000 years. Perhaps it was the late increase in human numbers or advancement of their hunting technology that tipped the balance there. However, most human habitations in Europe and Asia remained south of the woolly mammoth's main range in the millennia preceding its extinction; except occasionally and in small numbers, humans did not populate the Arctic until the present interglacial. Their role in decimating the original huge stocks of the mammoth can therefore be doubted.

In North America, the question of extinction is closely tied to the much-debated issue of when people first entered the continent. The first major archaeological evidence was left by people who entered North America across the Bering land connection from Siberia around 14,000 years ago, by 13,000 years ago spreading widely across the continent. The appearance of these 'Clovis' people corresponded closely in time to the extinction of the American mastodon, Columbian mammoth and other species, convincing many archaeologists that the Clovis people were responsible for megafaunal 'overkill'. There are intriguing hints of earlier humans in the Americas, however. The mastodon hunted at Manis, Washington State (see above), is dated to around 13,800 years ago – at least 800 years before Clovis. The decline in dung fungi in the northeast USA took place at a similar time and has been considered to be due to megafaunal population collapse caused by pre-Clovis human action, although this is speculative. Even earlier evidence has been proposed: at the Lovewell site in Kansas, broken mammoth bones were found together with an apparently artificially polished bone object dating to 22,000 years ago. Such early evidence of humans weakens the correlation of megafaunal extinction with the first human arrival, though it does not rule out a possible role for humans in the extinction.

The synergy of humans and climate

If neither climate change nor hunting alone seems likely to have caused the extinctions, the combination of them may have proved deadly. If populations of mammoth, mastodon and other megafauna had contracted to small areas due to the effects of climate change on their habitats, then hunting by prehistoric people could have tipped the balance. Although this implicates people in the extinction of the megafauna, it is a very different scenario from the idea that people alone were responsible for wiping out the mammoths and other species across their entire original ranges. The combined theory gives a major role to climate change but explains why extinctions did not occur during earlier such episodes. Then, mammal populations would also have been squeezed down to smaller numbers and areas, but, without the added impact of human hunting, most species survived to re-expand when conditions improved.

The vulnerability of small, isolated populations of animals is well known from threatened modern species (see below). There are various reasons why ssuch populations, restricted to 'islands' of remaining habitat, are at risk of extinction. Woolly mammoths, for example, were left on relatively small remaining areas of grassland habitat, without being able to migrate across larger areas of now unsuitable terrain (tundra or forest) to reach another suitable patch. In some cases, there was the danger of 'eating out' their food resource. A year or series of years of inclement weather affecting plant growth or water availability could knock the population back to numbers too small for it to recover. In other cases, human bands could have located isolated mammoth populations and wiped them out in relatively short measure.

The last two surviving populations of woolly mammoth provide likely examples of each of these modes – albeit in somewhat unusual circumstances as they were on real islands. The population of St Paul Island in the Aleutian chain west of Alaska expired some time after 6,500 years ago as the island area shrank due to rising sea levels until, at barely 100 km^2 (around 40 square miles), it was too small to sustain a mammoth population. There was no human involvement, as people did not reach the island until the eighteenth century. Wrangel Island, north of Siberia, is much larger, and supported a viable population of mammoths until, according to the genetic evidence (see above), they suddenly disappeared around 4,000 years ago. The earliest evidence of human presence on Wrangel is close in age to that of the last known mammoths, so it is possible that people arrived on the island to find a 'trapped' population of mammoths and rapidly hunted them to extinction. This remains speculative, however, as thus far we only have evidence of the early inhabitants hunting marine mammals such as walruses and seals, not mammoths.

Large mammals at risk

Whatever the cause or causes of their demise – habitat loss or hunting or both – the slow reproductive rate of the mammoths and mastodon counted against them. If their life cycles were similar to those of living elephants, females produced a single offspring only every 4 years or so. This factor may explain why the extinctions of the late Ice Age affected mostly larger species, since these generally have slower reproductive rates than smaller ones such as rodents or the small carnivores that feed on them. In consequence, the birth rate of their populations would have been insufficient to overcome an elevated death rate due to climate change or hunting. This effect would have been exacerbated if human hunters preferentially targeted larger species.

The loss of so many large mammals around the world has had a profound effect on today's ecosystems. It is not so much that Africa and Southeast Asia are unusual in preserving big game, as that the other continents are impoverished, with a lower diversity of large mammals than at any time over tens of millions of years. Ecologically, the lost biomass has been replaced, in effect, by humans and their domestic livestock. Some researchers have gone further and fear that the 'Ice Age' megafaunal extinction, now known to have extended to only 4,000 years ago when the woolly mammoth expired, represents the opening act of an ongoing, now human-caused destruction of the biosphere that may build into a mass extinction to rival those of the geological past.

THE FUTURE OF ELEPHANTS

Among the many species currently impacted by human action, the living elephants are increasingly under threat. From an estimated 5 million African elephants alive in the early twentieth century, only around 400,000–500,000 remain – a 90% loss. Asian elephants are more endangered still, with an estimated 40,000–50,000 remaining in the wild, plus 15,000 or so in captivity. The main causes of this decline have been on the one hand habitat loss, and, on the other, illegal killing (poaching). Both factors have impacted both species, with poaching probably the prominent factor for African elephants and habitat loss more greatly impacting the Asian elephant.

Elephant poaching

Elephants have been hunted by native peoples in Africa for millennia – but to a limited extent and mainly for the meat. This practice continues today, but has

RIGHT The forest elephant of Central and West Africa is smaller than the elephant of the open savannahs. It is currently in decline as a result of illegal hunting.

been greatly augmented by an international appetite for ivory, much of which is exported to countries of the Far East where carved ivory products remain popular. West Africa was the first region to suffer major reduction of its elephant population – it is no coincidence that one country was named the 'Ivory Coast' by its colonial rulers. As a result, most West African countries now count their elephants in tens or hundreds, with animals scattered in small blocks of isolated forest. Continent-wide, the killing reached a peak in the 1980s, when an estimated 100,000 African elephants were being killed per year, and up to 80% of herds were lost in some regions. In Kenya, the population plummeted by 85% between 1973 and 1989.

Asian elephants have been captured for domestic use for 4,000 years, but the systematic poaching of animals for ivory began only in the 1970s. In Asian elephants only the males may bear tusks, so poaching has resulted in a huge imbalance of males and females in certain areas, with up to 100 adult females for every adult male reported in one southern Indian population by the 1990s. In response to the slaughter, especially in Africa, the Convention on International

RIGHT A poached elephant lies on the African savannah. The tusks have been hacked from its head and its body left to rot.

RIGHT A poached elephant lies on the African savannah. The tusks have been hacked from its head and its body left to rot.

Trade in Endangered Species (CITES) in 1989 banned international trade in elephant ivory. This met with some success. Several countries in Africa experienced a steep decline in illegal killing, allowing their elephant populations to recover. In southern Africa, for example, elephant numbers have steadily increased and now stand at around 300,000 animals – three-quarters of the continent's total.

In countries with limited resources for wildlife protection, however, poaching continues. The currently worst-hit areas are in Central Africa, where elephants are now 'in crisis' according to a 2011 CITES report. There is a connection with illegal logging, since this opens routes into the dense tropical forest that allow access to wildlife poachers. As big tuskers are targeted, the average size of tusks has steadily decreased. Conservationists hoped that this would reduce the incentive for poachers to kill elephants, but the trade in bushmeat is sustaining the market, with smoked meat from one elephant fetching several hundred US dollars.

Habitat loss and fragmentation

As human populations expand, or as societies develop economically and increase consumption, they take up more and more land area, inhabiting and destroying the natural habitats where elephants and other wildlife live. The forest habitats of elephants in Asia and West Africa, for example, have been progressively eroded as land is cleared for settlements, crop-growing or livestock grazing. This leads to severe fragmentation of the elephant's habitat, so that once-large, mobile populations become trapped in small enclaves. Logged areas are sometimes left to form secondary growth of shrubs and grasses, creating a habitat which, although artificial, is actually attractive to elephants, leading to locally increased numbers of animals. As human populations increase past a certain density, however, elephant populations move away, though there may be nowhere suitable for them to re-establish in the region and their population will decline. In addition, traditional feeding or movement routes of elephants are often blocked by major roads, railways or overground pipelines. There is conflict as elephants invade settled or agricultural land, often destroying crops and buildings in the process, and sometimes killing people. Elephants may be killed in retaliation or as a preventative measure. Livestock compete with elephants for food, and may transmit diseases to the wild animals.

A final factor, likely to become more acute in the future, is climate change. The warming of global climate is creating complex changes in regional and local weather patterns, including temperature, rainfall and seasonal variation. These in turn cause the ranges of many plant and animal species to shift, so that community and habitat structure alter in a given area. For species like the elephant, whose populations are increasingly restricted to parks and reserves, climate change may render the habitat unsuitable for its inhabitants. Whereas in the past, animal species could often shift their ranges to track their preferred habitat, that habitat might no longer exist anywhere in the region, either because the climatic effects are too widespread, or because human activity has rendered all adjacent areas unsuitable for wildlife (e.g. because they are urbanized). While the nature and extent of this problem is as yet unknown for many areas of the elephants' range, it is a factor that wildlife managers and policy-makers need increasingly to incorporate within their planning.

LEFT Vast areas of tropical forest have been felled to make way for oil palm plantations, as in this aerial view of Sabah, Borneo.

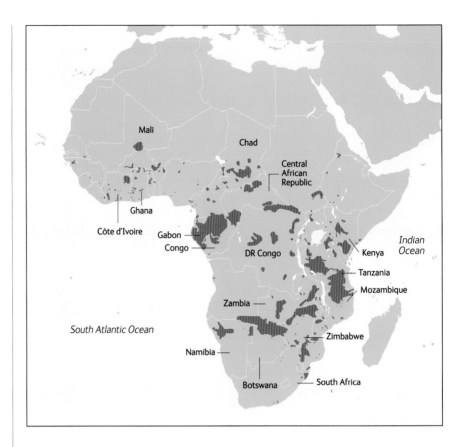

Conserving the elephants

Of the 200 or so species of proboscideans that have existed over the past 60 million years, only two remain (three if the African forest and savannah elephants are considered separate species). Their conservation therefore has high priority, if we wish to preserve as much of life's diversity as possible. Faced with a hard choice, the conservation of the last two members of an entire order of mammals takes precedence over two members of a group containing many similar species. Elephants are also considered 'flagship species' in that, requiring large areas of habitat to maintain a viable population, policies aiding their conservation inevitably preserve numerous other species of plants and animals as well. Finally, elephants are popular and iconic mammals with 'pulling power' in terms of charitable funding and persuading policy-makers of the political value of conservation.

The fragmentation of elephant populations is a major threat to their survival. After the decimation of African elephants in the 1980s, a study found that population size was closely related to survival potential: only 20% of populations occupying less than 250 km² (about 100 square miles) had survived, whereas for populations over 750 km² (about 300 square miles), 90% had survived. Recent computer modelling indicates that ideally a reserve size of several thousand square kilometres is required for long-term survival. With limited resources for

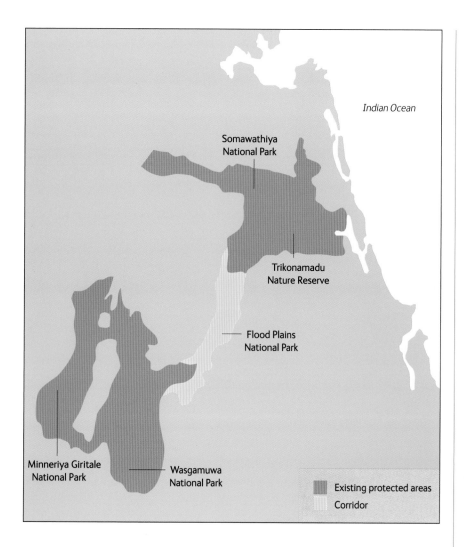

conservation, most effort therefore has to be placed on conserving the larger, more viable populations, although small populations may benefit from considerable attention in countries where they are the only elephants remaining. As well as the increased danger of total extermination from poaching, drought, disease or WAR habitat clearance, very small populations are also genetically vulnerable because of the negative effects of inbreeding on their health.

One solution to the problem of fragmented populations is to protect, strengthen or reinstate 'corridors' of natural habitat. Preferably at least 1 km (over ½ mile) wide, corridors allow animals to move freely between the areas, effectively combining two smaller populations into a larger one. Problems of human–elephant conflict are, however, complex and difficult to resolve. To keep out crop-raiding elephants, many communities dig trenches around agricultural land, or when resources allow, erect electric fences. The measures are of variable effectiveness. A potentially longer-term and more 'ecological' version is being trialled in Sri Lanka: a natural wall grown from closely planted rows of palm trees.

ABOVE Elephants destroy trees to obtain food, or to clear a pathway. Where elephant numbers are high in a restricted area such as a reserve, they can have significant impact on the landscape.

A further possible solution is the selective removal of particularly troublesome crop-raiding bulls. Where there is a decision to enlarge or create a protected area for elephants and other wildlife, whole villages have been moved outside the area and compensated for their trouble and financial loss. Conversely, the best solution for tiny elephant populations left stranded in the midst of human development may be to relocate the animals into an existing larger population.

The opposite problem applies in those areas where elephant populations have become unmanageably large for the limited area in which they can live. This is an artificial situation created by the restriction of populations to national parks. Elephant populations at high density destroy trees at a rate exceeding their capacity to regenerate, thus altering the landscape to the detriment of both the elephants and many other species. One proposed solution to the problem, the regular culling of elephants, has led to impassioned debate among conservationists. Culling programmes have been inaugurated in several countries, especially in southern Africa, with an average take of around 2,000 animals per year since the 1960s intended to keep populations in national parks at a stable, manageable level. Opponents argue that management policies such as the provisioning of artificial waterholes have contributed to the increased numbers of elephants, and that other factors, such as wildfires and giraffe grazing, impact tree growth as much as elephants. The elephants, left to their own devices, have natural cycles

of abundance and would regulate their own numbers. Opponents also consider the killing of such intelligent, social animals as morally repugnant. If carried out indiscriminately, the social fabric of the elephant society can be severely disrupted, for example by killing the experienced females known as matriarchs who lead the herd and retain knowledge of migration routes and feeding grounds.

ABOVE The Kenyan government in 1989 burnt its entire stockpile of tusks to draw attention to the rampant poaching of elephant populations. A year later CITES banned international trade in elephant ivory.

Poaching and the ivory trade

Tackling the hunting of elephants for meat or ivory has two components: preventing poaching on a local scale and cracking down on the international ivory trade. Most countries with elephants have patrols to enforce wildlife laws, but they are of variable effectiveness, often failing due to lack of resources or corruption among enforcement officers. Also, it is usually the hunters themselves who are caught, not gang leaders or dealers who will find others to replace lost personnel. The international community has to provide these countries with the resources as well as the political and economic incentives to effectively curtail their poaching problem. An international programme, Monitoring of Illegal Killing of Elephants (MIKE), is active in many areas, recording the degree of illegal hunting, noting any trends, and assessing the impact of outside factors such as international policy changes. It is thus able to provide the information needed by governments for the long-term management of their elephant populations.

ABOVE Hundreds of mammoth tusks are recovered from the Siberian permafrost every year. Many of them end up in ivory carving workshops alongside elephant tusks.

The international trade in ivory is an equally thorny issue. Far Eastern countries, which are the final destination of much of the world's poached ivory, as well as countries in Africa and the Middle East that act as staging-posts, have to redouble their efforts to stamp out illegal trading. The question of whether controlled legal sales should be allowed is a contentious one. The idea behind this policy is that countries with large elephant populations be allowed to sell ivory from legal culls or natural deaths, using the income to fund conservation efforts. Opponents, however, fear that anything fuelling the international ivory trade will sustain illegal killing of elephants. Kenya's public incineration of its entire stockpile of confiscated ivory in 1989 – 12 tonnes of tusks with a market value of US$ 3 million – was a dramatic statement of this position.

Extinct mammoths and endangered elephants

In a strange twist, the extinct woolly mammoth has become involved in the contentious issue of elephant ivory and conservation. The frozen remains of mammoths under the permafrost in Siberia and Alaska include large numbers of tusks. These comprise tusks still attached to partial or complete carcasses, as well as those which had become separated from the carcass before burial. Due to burial in permafrost, the tusks retain their original character and so are capable of being intricately carved. Starting in the eighteenth century, an industry of ivory excavation and export developed in Russia. The market continues today, the main producers claiming a turnover of 40–50 tonnes a year, corresponding to some 800 tusks or 400 mammoths. While some of it is carved and sold within Russia, most of it is exported. As the mammoth is an extinct species, it is not covered by CITES legislation, so such sales are legal in principle.

Questions have arisen as to the possible impact of this industry on the trade in elephant ivory, and ultimately on the poaching of living elephants. On the one hand, it might be supposed that by providing a 'replacement' to elephant ivory, mammoth ivory could reduce the need for the tusks of living elephants. On the other hand, it is argued that by keeping the ivory carving industry alive, it will bolster demand for the modern product too. Another concern is the laundering of illegal elephant ivory by marking or disguising it as mammoth ivory. Customs officers around the world have encountered this practice, but it is difficult to patrol because the difference between elephant and high-grade mammoth ivory is not always evident to the eye and requires chemical or DNA analysis, microscopic examination, or radiocarbon dating – all costly and time-consuming – for certainty. This has led to calls for the woolly mammoth to be the first extinct species whose trade is banned under CITES legislation.

Recent undercover surveys have investigated the degree to which the trade in mammoth ivory is a serious threat to the living elephants. At some trading centres in China, mammoth ivory objects were found to be as numerous as those of elephant ivory. Sales of both are increasing as China becomes more affluent and, worryingly, illegal elephant ivory is sometimes sold as mammoth in retail outlets. In Japan, by contrast, carvers dislike mammoth ivory, considering it harder and more brittle than recently gathered elephant ivory. Mammoth ivory can also be less economic for carvers because a certain amount has to be discarded if it

LEFT Beautiful objects can be carved from elephant and mammoth ivory – but at what cost?

RIGHT The last days of the woolly mammoth bear a striking resemblance to the current situation of the Asian elephant. Above, original mammoth range (purple) and latest records (orange). Below, historical Asian elephant range (purple) and current populations (orange).

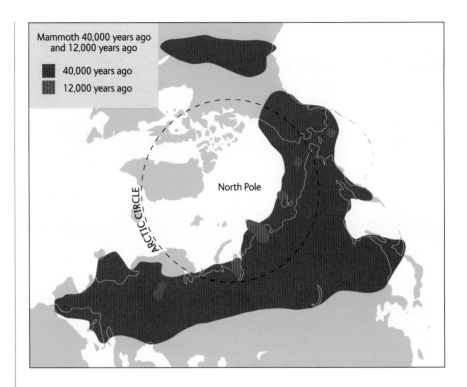

Mammoth 40,000 years ago and 12,000 years ago

■ 40,000 years ago
▦ 12,000 years ago

North Pole

ARCTIC CIRCLE

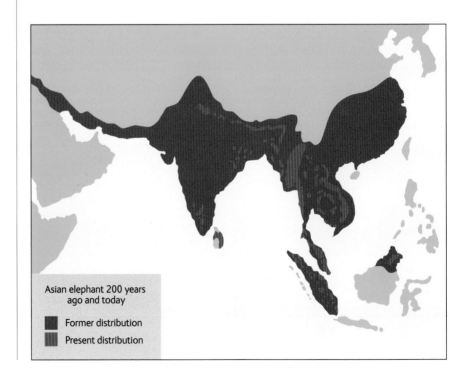

Asian elephant 200 years ago and today

■ Former distribution
▦ Present distribution

contains cracks or discoloration due to its long burial. The researchers concluded that at present there is no clear evidence that the mammoth ivory trade is either stimulating or depressing elephant poaching – in other words, if the sale of mammoth ivory were to be banned it would not alter the demand for modern ivory. More important is for consumer states to enforce their laws against illegal ivory and the disguising of elephant ivory as mammoth. However, they stress that the situation must continue to be monitored.

If the mammoth is unlikely to provide the means to save its living relatives, it at least gives a stark warning about the potential consequences of the threats they face. Our study of the mammoths' extinction has shown that it was the combined pressure of several factors that led to their demise. Those factors were climate change, habitat loss and hunting. It is evident that these are the same factors currently threatening the living elephants. The climate and habitat changes of the late Ice Age were naturally caused, whereas those being faced today and in the immediate future are the result of human action. The effect, however, is similar. In addition, again like the mammoth, remaining elephant populations are being eroded by the pressure of hunting, also known as poaching. Just as the mammoth saw a massive contraction of its range and numbers, and a fragmentation of its population into relict areas, so elephants, and many other species besides, are suffering the same fate. Our conclusion for the mammoth was that climate change and habitat loss reduced the species to relict populations, but might not alone have led to extinction. Hunting, conversely, was very unlikely by itself to have wiped out the entire original population. It was the combination of factors that was deadly. The multiple factors impacting elephants and other wildlife should therefore make it abundantly clear that we cannot afford to be complacent about the survival of these species, and must take action if we are to prevent their extinction. That is the lesson of the past to the present.

FURTHER INFORMATION

NB. Websites are correct at time of publication.

Chapter 1
Lister, A. and Bahn, P. *Mammoths: Giants of the Ice Age,* 3rd edition. Frances Lincoln, 2007.
van der Geer, A., Lyras, G., de Vos, J. and Dermitzakis, M. *Evolution of Island Mammals: Adaptation and Extinction of Placental Mammals on Islands.* Wiley-Blackwell, 2010.
Natural History Museum. http://www.nhm.ac.uk/nature-online/life/dinosaurs-other-extinct-creatures/dwarf-mammoth/

Chapter 2
Agusti, J. and Anton, M. *Mammoths, Sabertooths, and Hominids: 65 Million Years of Mammalian Evolution in Europe.* Columbia University Press, 2002.
Prothero, D. R. and Schoch, R. M. *Horns, Tusks, and Flippers: The Evolution of Hoofed Mammals.* Johns Hopkins University Press, 2002.
Savage, R. J. G. and Long, M. R. *Mammal Evolution: An Illustrated Guide.* British Museum (Natural History), 1986.
Shoshani, J. (ed). *Elephants.* Simon & Schuster, 1992.
About.com. http://dinosaurs.about.com/od/mesozoicmammals/a/elephants.htm

Chapter 3
Guthrie, R. D. *Frozen fauna of the Mammoth Steppe: The Story of Blue Babe.* University of Chicago Press, 1990.
Lange, I. M. *Ice Age Mammals of North America.* Mountain Press Publishing Company, 2002.
Lister, A. and Ursell, M. *The Ice Age Tracker's Guide.* Frances Lincoln, 2010.
Woodward, J. *The Ice Age: A Very Short Introduction.* Oxford University Press, 2014.
Wikipedia. http://en.wikipedia.org/wiki/Ice_age

Chapter 4
Haynes, G. *Mammoths, Mastodonts, and Elephants: Biology, Behavior and the Fossil Record.* Cambridge University Press, 1993.
Moss, C. *Elephant Memories: Thirteen Years in the Life of an Elephant Family.* University of Chicago Press, 2000.
Mueller, T. *Ice Baby: Secrets of a Frozen Mammoth. National Geographic,* May 2009, pp.30–55.
Sloan, C. *Baby Mammoth Mummy: Frozen in Time: A Prehistoric Animal's Journey Into the 21st Century.* National Geographic Society, 2011.
The Scientist. http://www.the-scientist.com/?articles.list/tagNo/3401/tags/ancient-DNA/

Chapter 5
Cook, J. *Ice Age art: arrival of the modern mind.* British Museum, 2013.
Levy, S. *Once and Future Giants: What Ice Age extinctions tell us about the fate of earth's largest mammals.* Oxford University Press, 2011.
Sukumar, R. *The Living Elephants: Evolutionary Ecology, Behaviour, and Conservation.* Oxford University Press, 2003.
World Wildlife Fund. http://worldwildlife.org/species/elephant

INDEX

ACKNOWLEDGEMENTS AND PICTURE CREDITS

Author's acknowledgements: I am most grateful to Dan Fisher, Georgi Markov, Simon Parfitt, Bill Sanders, Tony Stuart and Raman Sukumar for their very helpful comments and suggestions on the manuscript. I also warmly thank Harry Taylor for his superb photography of Natural History Museum specimens, and Trudy Brannan and Alessandra Serri for seeing the book through from conception to final product. Finally, I would like to personally thank those colleagues who have kindly provided personal research images for use in the book: Larry Agenbroad, Kevin Campbell, Vesna Dimitrijević, Dan Fisher, Victoria Herridge, George Iliopoulos, George Lyras, Dick Mol, Pavel Nikolskiy, Adam Rountrey and Evangelia Tsoukala.